FINDING
HEAVEN
HERE

First published by O Books, 2009
O Books is an imprint of John Hunt Publishing Ltd., The Bothy, Deershot Lodge, Park Lane, Ropley,
Hants, SO24 0BE, UK
office1@o-books.net
www.o-books.net

Distribution in:	South Africa
	Alternative Books
UK and Europe	altbook@peterhyde.co.za
Orca Book Services	Tel: 021 555 4027 Fax: 021 447 1430
orders@orcabookservices.co.uk	
Tel: 01202 665432 Fax: 01202 666219	Text copyright John C. Robinson 2008
Int. code (44)	www.johnrobinson.org
USA and Canada	Design: Stuart Davies
NBN	
custserv@nbnbooks.com	ISBN: 978 1 84694 156 6
Tel: 1 800 462 6420 Fax: 1 800 338 4550	

Australia and New Zealand
Brumby Books
sales@brumbybooks.com.au
Tel: 61 3 9761 5535 Fax: 61 3 9761 7095

Far East (offices in Singapore, Thailand,
Hong Kong, Taiwan)
Pansing Distribution Pte Ltd
kemal@pansing.com
Tel: 65 6319 9939 Fax: 65 6462 5761

Printed by Digital Book Print

O Books operates a distinctive and ethical publishing philosophy in
all areas of its business, from its global network of authors to
production and worldwide distribution.
This book is produced on FSC certified stock, within ISO14001
standards. The printer plants sufficient trees each year through
the Woodland Trust to absorb the level of emitted carbon in
its production.

FINDING HEAVEN HERE

Rev. John C. Robinson, Ph.D., D.Min.

BOOKS

Winchester, UK
Washington, USA

Finding Heaven Here *is a crash-course in spiritual transformation. In clear, compassionate terms, Dr. Robinson reveals the "secret" at the heart of all mystical traditions, and provides simple, practical exercises to bring it home to each and every reader. Required reading for anyone on a serious spiritual path.*
Rev. John R. Mabry, PhD, Author of *The Way of Thomas* and *Faith Styles*

The indigenous world embraces what the modern world has not yet grasped; heaven and hell, the extremities of our potential, exist in each moment, in the space between heartbeats, ready to take root in the fertile ground of intention and action. Finding Heaven Here, *then, one heartbeat away, is a response to the persistent drum call to cultivate and perpetuate sacred reality, here on earth.*
Malidoma Some, Author of *Of Water and Spirit, Ritual Healing and Community* and *Healing Wisdom of Africa*

John Robinson's elegant and moving examination of the universal human longing for 'heaven on earth' is a stirring demonstration of one of the most important precepts of interfaith ministry and theology: 'always in addition to, never instead of.'
Jeremy Taylor, author of *Dream Work, When People Fly and Water Runs Uphill,* and *The Living Labyrinth*

CONTENTS

ACKNOWLEDEMENTS

Finding Heaven Here is dedicated to my wife Mallow, my family, my friends – old and new – and to the world: May we all learn to live in the love and peace of Heaven on Earth.

I would also like to acknowledge the invaluable support, assistance and inspiration provided by Mathew Fox, Alexandra Kovats, and Carol Vaccariello of the University of Creation Spirituality (Wisdom University) in Oakland, the faculty and students of the Chaplaincy Institute for Arts and Interfaith Ministries in Berkeley, and mystic scholar and friend Andrew Harvey.

A Preview of Heaven on Earth

One day soon you will have an experience of Heaven on Earth. Perhaps this has happened already, but you didn't notice, you looked away or you've forgotten. Reading this book and using the exercises it provides might trigger an experience or make you aware of your past experiences of Heaven on Earth.

If you are not sure what experiencing Heaven on Earth might look or feel like, simply imagine your mind's incessant chatter falling silent and your awareness expanding, thus allowing you to discover a radiantly beautiful, exquisitely detailed, and utterly enchanting wonderland – imminently holy and infinitely precious – everywhere around you. Astonished, you examine one seemingly familiar thing after another, surprised to find each one transformed before your eyes into the most beautiful creation you have ever seen. Wonder and awe accompany you everywhere, and the world keeps growing more beautiful and extraordinary the longer you stay in this state of awareness.

"My God," you whisper, "This is amazing. It feels like I've just entered Heaven on Earth." (Indeed you have.)

Slowly and incredulously, it dawns on you that the whole universe has become alive, awake, and aware. A conscious Presence enfolds you – soft as sunlight, gentle, intimate, loving – and all your desperate everyday dramas evaporate in its peace. You realize, too, that this Presence creates and imbues all things – animate and inanimate alike – with its own life and consciousness: you, me, animals, trees, cities, homes, the Earth and the sky. With this knowing, you notice all things pulsing and vibrating with divine energy. People shine with the splendor of angels and Heaven's light transfigures reality right before your eyes. You understand that this omnipresent sacred consciousness – the answer to all problems, all questions, and all struggles – makes everything Heaven on Earth.

Rejoicing in the goodness, creativity, and love surging through Creation, doubts about purpose and worth vanish. You do not have to be good enough here; instead, Heaven on Earth invites you to explore the infinite possibilities of divine life.

And in Heaven on Earth, you discover that no place other than Heaven exists. Heaven on Earth lies here, wherever you are, right now, always full and always enough. Feelings of relief, gratitude, and joy nearly sweep you off your feet. You realize this is where you were meant to live — in Heaven on Earth. You are finally home.

Heaven on Earth awaits each of us. You've experienced it before, lived there in the past. Do you remember? Actually, you've never left Heaven on Earth; you've just forgotten how to see it. To do so, you need only to quiet your mind, heighten your awareness, and see the world anew in God's Presence. Come, let's go there together...

CHAPTER 1

The Story of Creation

"...this is it. This is Eden."
Joseph Campbell (Mythologist)

"Every prayer was fulfilled, every possible desire for the whole world consummated; for His Kingdom had come and I had beheld it with my very eyes."
Katharine Trevelyn (Mystic)

"On our notion of heaven may well rest the measure of the rest of our entire spiritual life."
Joan Chittister (Benedictine Sister, Author)

Introduction

Although the idea of Heaven on Earth seems as farfetched as Heaven itself, in actuality this "place" lies as close as sun sparkling on water on a pond outside your window, the gently moving branches of the trees in your yard or the sound of children laughing in the next room. From famous saints to everyday mystics, people from every religion and era have described Heaven on Earth from their own experience of it and you, too, can learn to see it.

The father's kingdom is spread out upon the earth and people do not see it.
Jesus (Christianity)

You might wonder where one finds Heaven on Earth. Is it hidden away in some long-forgotten valley, as portrayed in tales of

Shangri-La? Does one have to climb to the top of the highest peak to see it? No, but the best way to answer this question comes not from geography but from allegory. You see, Heaven on Earth arrives through a change of consciousness – a paradigm shift, if you will. It does not exist simply as a physical location. Allegories are the kind of stories that symbolize such transformation. In fact, the Judeo-Christian creation story provides a particularly good allegory for our purposes. Therefore, to help you understand where Heaven on Earth exists, I'd like to share with you a creative retelling of that story as a way of explaining the origin, nature and eventual disappearance of Heaven on Earth. The story goes like this:

This world is not the antechamber: it is the palace itself.
Levin Faitel (Judaism)

The Story of Creation
In the beginning, only Divinity existed as a realm unto itself: pure consciousness and potentiality. Wishing to know itself in a new way, the Divine burst forth in a fiery expansion of light and matter evolving the entire cosmos from its own essence. The Divine became the Universe and, in an act of infinite love and generosity, gave birth to a holy place called Earth. Divinity suffused everything with its own unique and unfolding nature (sea, rocks, plants, animals, weather, seasons). Thus Creation became a second divine realm – the physical world as a manifestation of Divinity.

Heaven is here on earth, and earth is there in Heaven.
Thich Nhat Hanh (Buddhism)

Among all the creatures that evolved from the Divine, one developed the unique capacity to think abstractly, to form concepts about the world and even to reflect on its own existence and relationship to the sacred. This creature was a part of Divinity becoming conscious of itself and of the

4

Universe – a wondrous epiphany. Thus, the human species came into being. In time, the human capacity for thought produced many marvelous inventions, including religion, agriculture, literature, architecture, science, engineering, medicine, and technology – a divinely inspired explosion of human creativity.

At the same time, however, something strange began to happen: Human beings became so fascinated with their concepts about the world that they began to mistake their concepts for the world itself. In other words, people increasingly saw only what they thought. Soon names, ideas, beliefs, and stories constructed a third and separate mental realm – the World of Man, and the sacred ground of Creation gradually disappeared from consciousness. Worse, entranced by the power of concepts, people began to view the natural world as simply a source of wealth or raw materials, a place to be conquered, controlled, used, and discarded. They stopped listening to the voices of Creation – such as the disappearing species, the shattered ecosystems and the displaced indigenous peoples – that spoke instead of damage, degradation and suffering.

This is the Kingdom of Heaven.
Ramana Maharshi (Hinduism)

Now at the center of humankind's third realm was the idea of self, a concept that became both a blessing and a curse. On the positive side, the self-concept allowed individuals to look within and discover much about their psychological and spiritual nature. On the negative side, however, the self-concept simply became too important. Humans became obsessed with this idea and soon everyone worried about the worth, goodness, beauty, power, wealth, and importance of the personal self. Tragically, this self-centeredness spawned ever-increasing competition, conflict and even warfare.

Living in the complicated World of Man, people increasingly betrayed and then forgot their divine nature and homeland, and this forgetting created a fourth and final realm: Darkness. It became a murky hidden space filled with the pain, anger and grief accumulated by each *new generation of children told to deny their divinity and believe instead that only the World of Man mattered. Those who felt this inner pain usually believed it was a sign of weakness and tried to overcome it by constantly improving their self-concept, or, if that failed, by finding ways to medicate the hurt into numbness. Some even pictured this Darkness to be far away in a horrible underworld called Hell. In either case, few wanted to visit this seemingly grim and gloomy landscape, not realizing that it was the World of Man, not Darkness, which had become increasingly grim and gloomy. Their tragic lack of understanding about this realm caused them to miss its precious gifts and opportunities. Yet, people's original divinity had not ceased to exist; this amazing, but greatly underutilized, source of healing and creativity simply lay hidden in Darkness.*

If on earth there be a paradise of bliss, it is this, it is this, it is this.

Firdausi (Sufism/Islam)

With diminishing joy, people in the World of Man concluded that they had been expelled from Creation. Some viewed this expulsion as divine punishment for their pursuit of knowledge, no longer remembering that humans had lost interest in the direct perception of Creation in the first place. Entranced by the power of the intellect and the grandiosity of the self, they had forgotten how to see the divine realm. Because they no longer witnessed or believed in Creation here on Earth, people erroneously imagined that both the Creator and the sacred world had relocated somewhere else, far away, in a place they called Heaven. That realm, they assumed, existed beyond this physical life.

Seduced by the imagined possibilities of self-importance, people decided that by acquiring enough wealth, power, fame, or perfection they still could find a substitute Heaven on Earth. As the World of Man grew ever more powerful, so did the forces of selfishness, greed, narcissism, and grandiosity.

As time went on, people occasionally would catch glimpses of the original world – for after all, Creation had never left and seeing it was still possible – but most, enmeshed in the World of Man, disbelieved their eyes and hurried on to the next problem, self-improvement project or grand activity. A few rare individuals, however, stopped to look more closely and realized that Heaven existed not just in the future but here, now, on Earth as well. More importantly, they discovered that whenever they sensed Divinity's Presence Heaven on Earth appeared all around them – in their gardens, families, and communities; Heaven was just another name for Creation. Some of these people became great mystics, prophets, or social activists. Others just lived in simple happiness or service. In either case, for these few the World of Man and its under-lying Darkness had become transparent, allowing them to see the radiance of eternity.

There is another heaven and earth beyond the world of men.
Li Po (Taoism)

Sadly, the vast majority of people in the world still failed to see Heaven on Earth and instead continued under the spell of destructive and erroneous beliefs. As a result, exploitation of nature and war between peoples continued, bringing the human species to the edge of extinction. The most desperate believed that only the apocalyptic end of the world itself would bring Heaven on Earth. Few understood that the future of humankind depended on all people finding and sharing Heaven on Earth right here, right now.

This revised creation story symbolizes humankind's journey away from the first-hand experience of Heaven on Earth as Creation itself to our current global crisis. This allegory also hints at how tremendously important it is for us to make the journey home to Heaven on Earth. In fact, survival in this fragile garden called Earth depends upon it.

> *Earth's crammed with heaven/And every common bush alive*
> *with God...*
> Elizabeth Barrett Browning (Poet)

A Word About the Word God

Having discussed the problem of concepts associated with the World of Man, it is probably a good time to talk about the concept of God. As a work on spirituality, *Finding Heaven Here* concerns itself directly with God. Unfortunately, we have so many names, images, and conceptions of God that the word itself can lead to confusion, debate, even conflict. For example, God may be conceived as masculine or feminine, life-giving or destructive, loving or punitive, and we often color the name with personal opinions or views from our own particular religion. While writing this book, someone advised me to substitute neutral phrases like "Ground of Being," "Pure Potentiality," or "Pure Consciousness" in place of God, which I often do, but they can also produce confusion along with the inevitable question, "Don't you mean God?"

> *The visionary sees the whole visible universe transfigured.*
> Evelyn Underhill (Religious Scholar)

In the end, I chose to refer to God simply as Divinity or Presence. For me, these terms are equivalent and interchangeable and refer not to an idea or belief but to the infinitely loving consciousness encountered in first-hand mystical experiences. Most importantly, please feel free to replace the words I have chosen with whatever word, phrase, or concept with which you're most comfortable, the one that gives your spirituality its sense of holiness, reverence, and meaning. And remember, this is a journey into the Divine not a comparative religions course. Whatever word you use for God ultimately should help you *experience* the Divine rather than intellectualize or debate it.

CHAPTER 2

Pilgrimage

Pilgrimage: (pil'gre-mij) n. A long journey, especially one made to a sacred place.
Funk and Wagnalls Standard Dictionary

The ordeal of being true to your own inner way must stand high in the list of ordeals. It is like being in the power of someone you cannot reach, know, or move, but who never lets you go; who both insists that you accept yourself and who seems to know who you are.
Florida Scott-Maxwell (85 y/o Jungian Analyst)

All theology, like all fiction, is at heart autobiography.
Frederick Buechner (Professor of Religion, Author)

Introduction

Despite the compelling views and convictions of the World of Man, Heaven on Earth remains an ever-present and all pervasive reality shining in everything. Although this chapter tells the story of my pilgrimage to Heaven on Earth, it also speaks of our common struggle to see the world again with new eyes, eyes able to see Divinity in everything. I found Heaven on Earth, and so can you.

As you read this chapter, indeed as you read the whole book, I make one request: Take it seriously. The cynic rarely finds Heaven on Earth while the motivated seeker who approaches Heaven with an open mind and heart finds it everywhere. If you limit your vision with negative beliefs, you'll miss the magic this book has to offer.

A Psychologist's Spiritual Journey

I have been searching for Heaven on Earth my whole life, following an invisible compass setting that would never let me go. Whenever I strayed too far afield from this setting, I felt restless, lost, or discouraged. Sometimes, on the other hand, when feeling especially peaceful, rested, or centered, an indecipherable joy would erupt inside – an intuition of a place I already knew but could not quite identify. This unyielding compass led me through countless spiritual writers, practices and experiences. It has driven my writing and pushed me relentlessly past traditional dogma and beliefs. Long before I knew what I was searching for, this unseen arrow held my course and knew its destination. Then, at long last, I realized where I was going and why.

I am a retired clinical psychologist. I spent nine years in college and graduate school studying the nature, causes, and treatment of psychological disorders and three decades working in the profession in numerous settings and capacities. Although I learned a great deal about the psychological basis of human suffering, my understanding always felt incomplete. In my heart of hearts I knew there was something missing – something fundamentally spiritual about our suffering and our joy, a dimension of reality as important and verifiable as anything psychology studied. Only recently did I realize that this spiritual dimension was the experience of Heaven on Earth. Let me explain how I arrived at this realization.

As a child, I sensed a pervasive, radiantly beautiful, living mystical reality shining all around me. Running in summer sunshine, bare feet on grass wet with morning dew, myself and all things bursting with the energy, consciousness, and joy of Creation, life felt too full to contain. Spirit filled the world with implicit love, its light illuminating natural beauty like a colorful stained-glass window, its presence a great invisible tide moving through everything. Though at the time I couldn't express these sentiments in adult words, I remember the joy of this experience nearly lifting my feet off the ground.

Because clarity and enlightenment are within your own
nature, they are regained without moving an inch.
Lao Tzu (Taoist Sage)

Meandering through grassy fields like a mystical explorer, I touched rough-hewn bark, studied daffodils and smelled the subtle fragrances of earthy flowerbeds in the noonday heat. Birds' songs virtually hypnotized me with their sweet melodies. Everything appeared precious and timeless, and I had no thought of yesterday or tomorrow. I adored – almost worshipped -- my mother and father for their magnificent beauty, natural charisma and angelic presence. Everything seemed fascinating, perfect, spacious, and complete and I unquestionably assumed this wonderland would be mine forever.

Then, gradually, insidiously but insistently, beliefs and expectations from the World of Man descended upon my bright and colorful existence. For example, it dawned on me one day that love had become conditional. Shocked and amazed, I realized that people – even parents – create fixed judgments of you based on some snippet of behavior, and these judgments can determine how much they love or want you.

Standing in the living room one day, I watched my older brother pretend to conduct a symphony with remarkable mastery and flair. He obviously knew things that I didn't, things that apparently made him admirable and important in the eyes of family and society. Even my mother stopped working in the kitchen to watch in awe and pleasure. I had nothing comparable to show for myself. Instead, in an outburst of jealousy and envy, I pushed my little brother, for whom love had not yet become conditional, to the ground simply for being younger.

"I've had it with you," my mother shouted angrily, and banished me to my room. Suddenly, my parents considered me a problem child. I felt puzzled, angry and frightened by these new and nonnegotiable rules concerning their love. Worse, I realized that adults had little or no interest in the divine world. Busy with tasks, schedules and conversations, they rarely stopped to appreciate the inexhaustible beauty I witnessed everywhere. "Why is this happening?" I wondered, as I watched adult concepts about behavior and personal value infect siblings and friends like a contagious illness.

In a broad sense, the Bible as a whole is the story of the dream of God, beginning with Paradise and ending with Paradise restored in the great concluding vision of the book of Revelation.
Marcus Borg (Profession of Religion and Culture, Author)

Over the ensuing years, I felt repeatedly saddened as those around me exchanged the divine world for these new worries about self worth. A protective numbness, however, soon moved over my soul and I shut down emotionally and spiritually. Looking back, of course, I realize that my experience represented the universal fall from grace – the magic of Creation – into the World of Man with its conceptual grid of beliefs, rules, and expectations.

The years I spent in middle school proved an especially hard period for me. As old friends tried on new identities, competing in games of popularity and discarding undesirables like trash, I felt alone and naked. I didn't want to wear an identity but felt vulnerable without one. During the same period, I suffered the unexpected trauma of open-heart surgery to correct a birth defect. When I awoke from the anesthesia, I wondered, "Where was the joy of the bright world now?"

Unfortunately, I found no safe space in which to ask my questions and no one to provide me with the answers I sought. I realized that if I wanted to make it in the World of Man, if I wanted the conditional love and belonging it offers, I must become a player or go into hiding. I became a player – we all do sooner or later. Of course moments of love and wonder broke through along the way like sunshine through dark clouds, but the World of Man kept encroaching until it became my way of life.

Now some of you may consider these examples silly or childish. "Everyone has to grow up," you might argue, "get over it. It's about taking responsibility for yourself. You don't get taken care of like a child forever." And you would be correct, of course, but you would also miss a more subtle point. The fear and worry generated by these ideas exile us from Heaven on Earth. We can spend a lifetime worrying about personal worth, survival and love, and, as a result, never return to the Garden.

Since the Fall, we tend to be over involved in a man-made world we have superimposed on creation.
Adrian van Kaam (Professor of Spirituality, Author)

Despite the disappointment and grief that kept growing in my inner Darkness, I never stopped searching for the bright world I had lost. My home office overflowed with books on religion, spirituality and mysticism, as if I tacitly knew that the way back to Creation had something to do with these subjects and that the information I needed could be found somewhere between their covers.

Years passed. Then, one evening in midlife, I read the following account of one man's mystical experience in William Stace's "Mysticism and Philosophy":

The room in which I was standing looked out onto the backyards of a tenement. The buildings were decrepit and ugly, the ground covered with boards, rags, and debris. Suddenly every object in my field of vision took on a curious and intense kind of existence of its own...And every object, seen under this aspect, appeared exceeding beautiful. There was a cat out there with its head lifted, effortlessly watching a wasp that moved without moving just above its head.

Everything was urgent with life...which was the same in the cat, the wasp and the broken bottles, and merely manifested itself differently in these individuals...All things seemed to glow with a light that came from within them...

I experienced a complete certainty that at that moment I saw things as they really were, and I was filled with grief at the realization of the real situation of human beings, living continuously in the midst of all this without being aware of it. This thought filled my mind, and I wept. But I also wept over the things, themselves, which we never saw and which we made ugly in our ignorance...

My immediate reflections on the experience at the window were as follows: I saw how absurd had been my expectations of a vision of God... For I had no doubt that I had seen God...it turned out to be the world that I looked at everyday...As Blake put it, 'all life is holy' and that is enough; even the desire for more seems to me more spiritual greed. It is enough that things are, a man who is not content with what is simply does not know what is.

I put the book down and stood by the bedroom window for a long time, stunned and speechless, as if the Earth had suddenly stopped spinning. Then I understood. In his mystical experience, this man had actually witnessed the divine world: radiantly beautiful, literally alive, and always present despite our failure to see it – and the place he described was the place I had known as a child.

Barely able to contain my excitement, I reread his description countless times, tried to explain its astounding significance to my wife and eventually collected hundreds of similar accounts from friends, clients and the spiritual literature. I knew now that the mystical experience was humankind's truest perception of the world and, as such, represented the most important insight in religion and spirituality since Jesus proclaimed the coming of the Kingdom of God. Moreover, the account I read in Stace's book had uncovered the secret hidden in my soul since childhood: Life's purpose lies in finding and living in the radiant divine reality revealed by the mystical experience.

Searching For Heaven

The search for Heaven on Earth now consumed me, and, as a result, gifts of guidance, insight and revelation began arriving daily. When you knock on Heaven's door, it opens.

I was in the process of writing a book for mental health professionals on the integration of psychotherapy and spirituality when a diagram of humanity's essential spiritual struggle took shape in my mind like an image appearing in a psychic's crystal ball. For several years I worked and reworked its meaning and implications, and, in doing so, my lifelong spiritual search – and my invisible compass – started to make sense. I realized that the World of Man had completely distracted me from the presence of Heaven on Earth and Divinity itself. The resulting Darkness hid my pain, my sacredness and my way back to Heaven on Earth. This diagram, which I present and explain in Chapter 4, also showed me that by learning to experience Divinity directly I could rediscover Heaven on Earth again. The path to my destination cleared, and my invisible compass arrow pointed directly to Heaven. Thus, I called this first gift Heaven's Compass.

The second gift turned out to be even more dramatic. It arrived while working on a book of spiritual exercises for experiencing Divinity directly. As if guided from above, I kept creating what I later called "experiments in consciousness," processes meant to sharpen our natural mystical sensitivity for God's Presence. Since the mystics from across traditions consistently have said God lies beyond ideas and beliefs, I developed one experiment that involved examining reality with intentionally heightened and thoughtless awareness. Wide-eyed and wide awake, I would stare intensely at something – a book, a lamp, a flower, my hand – until its sensory qualities became hyper-real, exquisitely detailed and beautiful, exceptionally bright and colorful. I saw how the ever-present lens of thought had in the past filtered out the object's captivating beauty and said to myself, "The world is completely different than what we think and far more amazing." This observation fit perfectly with the mystical experience quoted above and suggested to me that anyone could learn to see the divine world intentionally.

Since I intuitively sensed that all consciousness really belongs to God, another exercise I created focused on becoming conscious of consciousness itself. As I practiced this exercise, an alchemical reaction began to simmer inside of me; my formerly clouded consciousness gradually burned away to expose an unfiltered and sharper way of seeing.

Like most people, I always had considered consciousness – the experience of being awake and aware – as arising from biological functions associated with the brain and, therefore, belonging to the individual. In other words, I assumed consciousness existed inside, rather than outside, each person and that my consciousness was separate from everyone else's consciousness.

One day, however, while combining the two experiments described above, I developed a remarkable new awareness. Suddenly I experienced consciousness everywhere. It was not in me; I was in it. Moreover, I acquired the capacity to experience an omniscient divine awareness all around me, and I now could feel its incredible tenderness, kindness and love. In this heightened and awakened consciousness, the world itself changed. Everywhere I looked the things I saw shone with newness, clarity and luster as if they had just been created.

I could hardly believe my eyes. The beauty, perfection and wonder of my childhood divine world had returned. Once again I walked in a bright wonderland of extraordinary sights, colors, smells, and sounds. For me, such things as green leaves in speckled morning light shining through dusty windows now held all the hushed holiness of a magnificent stained glass window in a famous cathedral.

Astonished and enthralled, I practiced these experiments at

home, in stores, at work, and outside. I understood that this omnipresent consciousness belonged to God and marveled at its power to transfigure reality before my eyes, peeling away the ugliness I normally saw in the world like old paint to reveal a radiant paradise beneath. Now Heaven on Earth appeared everywhere.

I created a third experiment in consciousness that involved tuning into the pure physical energy of my body. I wanted to sense that energy unfiltered by customary physical labels, such as tension, aches, pains, itches, or the emotional language of feelings, such as excited, happy, or sad. To my amazement, just as Hindu and Buddhist mystics foretold, in that pure experience of being I found the origin of bliss. The deeper I felt my own being, the greater the ecstasy I experienced until I could no longer contain the intensity of joy and consciously would choose to stop the process.

> *What is bliss but your own being? You are not apart from being which is the same as bliss.*
> Ramana Maharshi (Hindu Sage)

In addition, I realized that the apparent separation I perceived between myself and God was caused by identity-related concepts like "me," "mine" and "God." I understood that such concepts actually divide up the mystical oneness of Being – the unity described by every great religion – into seemingly separate and distinct objects and processes. Thus, by definition, my identity differed from God's identity; hence God and I could not be the same. When I ceased experiencing the world through concepts, the distinction between "me" and "God" dissolved naturally and progressively into that mystical unity, and I knew first hand that we are all One. In temporarily melting into Divinity, I had experienced the divine union touted by saints and mystics, yet this oneness turned out to be no more unusual than sitting happily in the sunshine feeling the joy of just being alive. Amazingly, I had always been this close to God.

Looking back, I realize that all these experiments in consciousness involved undoing the mental and perceptual habits that had caused me to lose sight of Heaven on Earth in the first place. A thick lens of thoughts, concepts and beliefs had overridden my simple perception of the divine world. For example, preconceptions automatically reduced a chair from a living pulsing extension of Divinity to a piece of "furniture." Likewise, rather than being an amazing flow of conscious blissful energy, I became a "person" with various culturally defined "problems" in need of fixing. I viewed the world not as a Heavenly landscape of angelic beings and radiant beauty but a place of upsets, problems, negativity, suffering, and unhappiness. My beliefs created and projected an ugly reality and my eyes perceived that reality.

The development of spiritual consciousness begins when we release all concepts of God in the recognition that the I that is seeking God is God.
Joel Goldsmith (Author)

The next gift from the universe came attached to a puzzling problem. I found myself stumbling upon references to Heaven on Earth everywhere in my reading, which I saw as signs of divine encouragement and confirmation. It seemed to me the time had finally come for this idea to germinate in humankind's collective consciousness, but no one pursued its extraordinary implications. Instead of describing the imminent beauty of Heaven on Earth and encouraging readers to experience it, each writer simply touched on the subject and then went on to another one.

Certain that readers would be interested in a book on Heaven on Earth, I decided to pursue publication of an earlier manuscript I had written on this topic, but publishers I approached rejected it. Shocked and disheartened, I wondered why such a profound and important revelation could be so casually disregarded. Then I realized again the power of cynical and negative beliefs: The possibility of Heaven on Earth was still inconceivable to authors and editors alike. If they couldn't conceive this glorious reality, or more importantly, if they couldn't see it, then readers would never hear about it.

Happily, things were quite different in the classes I had been teaching on Heaven's Compass for several years in a spirituality program at a large Catholic retreat center. I had incorporated my experiments in consciousness into the course, and my students found that using these exercises created a powerful tool for transforming personal problems into glimpses of Heaven on Earth. Countless times I witnessed participants' troubled stories and emotions replaced by the wisdom and joy of Divinity and its Creation simply by using these exercises. The manuscript received similarly positive responses from faculty and peers when it evolved into a dissertation for a Doctor of Ministry degree. Thus, despite this publishing setback, my confidence in my perceptions of Heaven on Earth and ability to reveal it to others grew stronger. All the while, as the alchemy of change simmered inside, my life quietly transformed.

The Final Challenge

Before I could make the great leap forward into Heaven on Earth, however, I had to learn one very personal, powerful and shocking lesson, and without Heaven's Compass, I might not have survived this lesson at all. In June of 2000, after a long and tiring day of doing psychotherapy, my heart began to beat erratically, and this atrial fibrillation sent me to the emergency room. Shortly after being defibrillated (having an electrical shock applied to my chest to make my heart beat regularly again), I began experiencing repressed memories of my childhood open-heart surgery. As the memories intensified, I could actually feel the knife cutting through my chest wall, hands working inside my heart, and the sheer horror of being splayed open in the cold, dark, timelessness of surgical paralysis.

By reviewing the literature on anesthesia awareness and talking to several prominent researchers in the field, I learned that people sometimes wake up in surgery. Somewhere between 40,000 to 140,000 times a year in American operating rooms, anesthesia levels drop too low to maintain a patient's unconsciousness. Thus, these patients wake up during the surgery but remain chemically immobilized, which prevents them from being able to communicate this terrifying situation to their surgeon or to the operating-room staff. Some patients emerge from this experience in states of acute psychological trauma. Others repress the unbearable trauma and may not experience it until months or even years later.

To my horror, I realized that I had begun to remember – and to relive – a surgical nightmare that had so devastated me 40 years earlier that I had suppressed all memories of it ever having happened at all. In time, the rapidly escalating recollections became so painful and distracting that I was forced to close my psychology practice. I found it impossible to listen to my patients' problems while experiencing open-heart surgery going on in my body at the same time. My suffering became so unbearable that I had to devote the limited energy I had to my own healing.

This work in our souls cannot be accomplished by cleverness, intelligence, or any subtlety of mind, but only by completely abandoning ourselves to the divine action, becoming like metal poured into a mold, or a canvas waiting for the brush, or marble under the sculptor's hands.
Jean-Pierre de Caussade (18th Century Jesuit Theologian)

I worked through this trauma in psychotherapy, which entailed a long, slow process of re-experiencing and releasing the emotions associated with each horrific memory. With the aid of Heaven's Compass, I also worked on the trauma spiritually. Using exercises

I had taught in my classes, Heaven's Compass helped me heal and release these memories of anesthesia awareness by moving me from the hell of trauma back to Heaven on Earth. During the process, Heaven's Compass also became a source of revelations, providing me with countless insights about the spiritual journey.

First, I learned that hell is created by the stories we tell. The only story I had at the time of my surgery was a terrible one: I thought I was being dissected alive and that no one cared that I felt it occurring. Second, I learned that any hell, no matter its nature or origin, eventually dissolves in the peace of Presence. That said, accomplishing this goal of melting hellish memories in the healing experience of Presence may take a lot of practice, because the traumatic stories we create, and our attachment to them, go deeper than we realize. Third, I learned that Heaven never goes away – we do. Thus, we must learn to return over and over and never give up our effort to find our way home to Heaven on Earth.

In addition, this event reminded me that Darkness holds the wounded self, and without the soul-recovering journey into its pain, we cannot proceed to Heaven on Earth. Whatever remains incomplete in our past has the power to stall our current journey. In my case, part of me lay frozen in the coldness of surgery, shattered, numb, and discarded, and I had to retrieve and love the 14-year-old boy to restore his – and my – life. Without responding to this split-off self with reassurance, sensitivity, and deep love, he would have remained imprisoned in the Darkness of the unconscious, and therefore so would I.

I also became aware that the final resolution of trauma lies not just in healing the traumatic story, but moving beyond stories altogether – including your personal narrative – into divine consciousness. Stories, the fictions we tell ourselves to explain our lives and problems, are part of the conceptual World of Man. Until we learn to dissolve them in the experience of God's Presence, they too will obscure our view of Heaven on Earth. For example, even saying, "I am healed" creates a new set of ideas, explanations and fantasies adding to the thought-wall blocking my perception of the divine world. We get distracted so easily by the stories we believe and tell the world.

Finally I learned that God enters our lives through sudden and unexpected events to change our world forever. The event may arrive as a car accident, job loss, divorce, or a thousand other possibilities, but you realize in that moment that you cannot save the old order of things and must begin to let go of all you once knew. My event, cardiac defibrillation, took my vocation, income and identity. Sometime later, however, possibilities of renewal begin to arrive on our doorstep. Indeed we are presented with a new path, no longer linear or logical, no longer tied to our former plans or identity – and inevitably involving service to the world. That's why God punches our tickets. In my case, I no longer work as a psychologist; instead I have begun a life of service devoted to revealing and sharing Heaven on Earth.

Living in Heaven on Earth

I have learned to reside more and more now in the silent and awakened consciousness of Presence and the divine world it illuminates. In this consciousness, I recognize concepts and beliefs as the source of duality, confusion, and suffering. A new kind of life has begun as I witness what the Bible alludes to as a "new Heaven and new Earth" (Isaiah 65:17, Revelation 21:1), that is, a new heavenly consciousness and the divine realm it reveals, a life available to all of us when we finally learn to see. With Heaven's Compass as our guide, you, too, can discover where you really live and what really blocks your path to eternity. We all were born to know Heaven in this lifetime. Like me, you can know it, too. If you are willing and open to the experience, come with me now. Find Heaven here.

CHAPTER 3

The Promise

*Jacob woke from his sleep and said, 'Truly the Lord is in this place,
and I did not know it...This is no other than the house of God, this is
the gate of heaven.'*
The Bible (Genesis)

*I believe in heaven! But I don't believe in heaven as a place somewhere
else. Heaven is everything transfigured by God's presence.*
David Steindl-Rast (Benedictine Brother, Author)

*"Am I 'going to heaven'? No, I am already there and it is getting more
heavenly everyday."*
Joan Chittister (Benedictine Sister, Author)

Introduction

The world's voluminous spiritual literature bursts with mystics,
scholars and everyday folks asserting not only that Heaven can
be found but that it can be found right here. These are not a
wacky bunch of true believers; they represent a cross-section of
people from around the world with different backgrounds and
diverse religious traditions. To assure you that I am not some
weirdo with a far-out and unbelievable idea about Heaven on
Earth, this chapter presents an anthology of their claims – which,
of course, support my premise – grouped somewhat arbitrarily
into the following categories: religion, mythology, archeology,
naturalism, etymology, poetry, mystical experiences, ordinary
experiences, and aging. Enjoy this banquet of testaments to the
continued existence of Heaven on Earth. (Original sources and
additional quotations can be found in the Appendix A.)

Religion

The world's religions provide the most obvious place to look for descriptions of Heaven on Earth, and they have included some of the most determined mystics seeking first-hand experiences of the Divine. Not surprisingly, I found remarkable agreement among these mystics' testimony.

This is the essential message of all religion. The infinite, transcendent, holy Mystery, which is what is signified by 'God' or 'Heaven', is present in the world... The Kingdom is universal... It has existed from the beginning, in all times and in all places.
Bede Griffiths (Catholic Monk, Hindu Scholar, Author)

Judaism: In the Torah, Heaven on Earth takes the form of Eden, which in Hebrew means "place of delight." In the Garden of Eden, believed to be an actual paradise on Earth, the first human beings dwelled in God's presence without self-consciousness, worry or suffering. God expelled them from the Garden, however, for eating from the tree of the knowledge of good and evil. In this creation story, therefore, we first lived in Heaven on Earth.

Psychologists have long suggested that creation myths may symbolize the evolution of human consciousness. Interpreted symbolically therefore, it might be said that as human beings began conceptualizing themselves and their lives – particularly in dualistic terms such as good-evil and right-wrong – they replaced the consciousness of Creation with the World of Man. This process of replacing perception with cognition, of course, happens both in personal development as well as in the evolution of culture.

Moreover, according to Miriam Van Scott, author of the comprehensive "Encyclopedia of Heaven," expectations of the Garden's return also characterized Jewish thinking centuries before Jesus proclaimed the Kingdom of God. Thus, Judaism anticipates humanity's eventual rediscovery of the divine world. In fact, Hebrew Scriptures suggest that the perception of Heaven on Earth returns each time someone transforms consciousness in the presence of Divinity, as when Jacob awoke from a dream encounter with God to discover that he was standing at the "gate of heaven." Rabbi Noah Weinberg, the founder of Aish HaTorah International, adds that God also transforms Shabbat, Judaism's holy day, into "a taste of Heaven on Earth" by intensifying the spiritual level of the world.

The Jewish mystical tradition of the Kabbalah, which emerged in the twelfth and thirteenth centuries, contains more specific suggestions that Heaven can be found here. For example, Daniel Matt, author of "The Essential Kabbalah," tells us that kabbalists view the Garden of Eden as the origin of mystical knowledge. They further believe our original nature shares the pure, uncorrupted consciousness of Adam and Eve, and Eden continues to flow into the ordinary world. Indeed, David Sheinkin, author of "The Path of the Kabbalah," asserts that to kabbalists, the spiritual world stands "right in front of us."

The kabbalist Yehuda Berg explains it this way. God split reality into two realms. The first contains the blazing Light of eternity filled with knowledge, wisdom, and joy that flows from the Divine. The much smaller physical world perceived by our senses constitutes the second realm. Ten curtains divide these two realms, each one progressively diminishing the Light. Matt's translation of the scripture of Kabbalah suggests that rather than concealing the divine Light, these curtains actually serve to reveal its presence, as when cloth covering an intensely bright lamp allows the light to shine through. In sum, with the Light of eternity permeating everything, Heaven literally fills the Earth. Our work as human beings, the Kabbalah further instructs, involves drawing forth this Light to achieve the world's divine potential. Through our devotion to religious practice, we bring Heaven and Earth together.

Rabbis from the Lubavitch Hasidus movement, the best-known branch of Hasidic Jewry, have been even more articulate in describing the experience of Heaven on Earth. According to Michael Levin, Rabbi Zalman, the founder of this movement, argued that the goal of religion was not just to attain Heaven in the afterlife but to "achieve a taste of heaven on Earth." In fact, some from this movement believe that devotion to study actually leads to the attainment of paradise. In his book, "Heaven on Earth," Faitel Levin adds that there is no need to transcend the world. The ultimate communion with God takes place here, for "the *essence* of this reality is nothing but the Essence of God." He concludes, "This world is not an antechamber: it is the palace itself."

Christianity: Heaven on Earth becomes an even more distinct reality in the words of Jesus and later Christian writers. The New Testament refers to Heaven on Earth as the Kingdom of God, and many Christians believe it will arrive only after Armageddon, a time during which the evil world created by humankind is destroyed and replaced by the perfection of the heavenly Jerusalem. However, some translations of the "Gospel of Luke" suggest that the Kingdom already exists among us, and in the "Gospel of Thomas," Jesus says that Heaven is spread all over Earth but men do not see it.

Joseph Campbell, the famous scholar of world mythology and religion, explains that these statements mean the experience of Heaven, here and now, requires only a transformation of consciousness, not the literal end of the world. He asserts, "This is Eden. When you see the kingdom spread upon the earth, the old way of living in the world is annihilated. The end of the world is not an event to come; it is an event of psychological transformation, of visionary transformation."

Authors Morton Kelsey and John Sanford, writing from a Christian-Jungian orientation, further suggest that the Heaven of which Jesus spoke is both immanent and transcendent. In other words, it exists both here and in the hereafter. Heaven on Earth, they conclude, is a present spiritual reality that can be known directly. Numerous others add that mystics experience Heaven and Earth as the very same place, a place literally transfigured by the experience of God's Presence.

Union with God makes the earth a paradise once more. Where God is with me, there is paradise and the whole of nature is the lovely background to our friendship...For those who live in union with God all things are transfigured by a special light, and joy springs from them - even the most common everyday things. Blessedness falls on every moment of their life and there is a kind of enchantment upon everything they touch, everything they do.
Ernesto Cardenal (Nicaraguan Priest and Poet)

Andrew Harvey, a mystic and author, concludes, "We all long for heaven where God is, but we have it in our power to be in heaven with Him at this very moment." Indeed, Colleen McDannell and Bernhard Lang, authors of "Heaven, A History," suggest that we glimpse Heaven on Earth all the time and should aspire to increase such incidents rather than being preoccupied with reaching Heaven in the afterlife. Even modern day psychic, Edgar Cayce, instructs, "That which would prevent our knowing where heaven is, is in ourselves only," for heaven is "all about us," a sentiment further echoed by modern spiritual teacher Caroline Myss who summarized, "Heaven walks next to you."

Heaven on Earth finds another welcome home in the Creation Spirituality theology of Matthew Fox, author of 26 books on the subject. After quoting the Catholic saint Julian of Norwich – "We are more truly in heaven than on earth" – Fox tells us that Jesus' essential message proclaimed that the Kingdom had already arrived, a message echoed in the work of Meister Eckhart, the medieval theologian and mystic. "The kingdom is here," Eckhart declares, "when we are awake enough to see it." More importantly, Fox says, "...if heaven has not already begun for us it is our dualistic way of envisioning our lives that is the major obstacle..." Calling this message "realized eschatology," Fox summarizes, "Now is the time, Now is the place...Now is the moment of divine breakthrough."

The experience of Heaven on Earth has also been repeatedly described by Christian mystics. Over 200 years ago, the English poet and mystic William Blake promised that if the "doors of perception" were cleansed, we would see the infinite standing directly before us. Jacob Boehm, a German shoemaker transformed by a profound mystical experience in 1600, confirmed, "Heaven is throughout the whole World...It filleth all...without division," but added, "Men seek and find not, because they seek it not in the naked Ground where it lieth; but in something or other where it never will be, nor can be." Similarly, Thomas Traherne, a seventeenth century mystic, recalled vivid memories of Heaven on Earth from childhood, concluding, "Certainly Adam in Paradise had not more sweet and curious apprehensions of the world, than I when I was a child."

Your enjoyment of the world is never right, till every morning you awake in Heaven; see yourself in your Father's Palace... The world is a mirror of infinite beauty, yet no man sees it. It is a Temple of Majesty, yet no man regards it. It is a region of Light and Peace, did not men disquiet it. It is the Paradise of God...It is the place of Angels and Gate of Heaven.
Thomas Traherne (Mystic)

Finally, Robert Keck, a United Methodist minister, suggests that the chaos of our present era represents a transformation of humanity's collective consciousness leading to a third and final era of human spiritual evolution. He characterizes this era as the "spirituality of time" in which "Heaven and earth are one. Human and divine are one." Keck concludes, "Eternity is available for us right now, right here, spread throughout the earth, inside us, and all around us. We need simply to awaken...to the ever-present heaven, the eternal now."

Hinduism: Some of the greatest contemporary teachers of Hinduism have said that whoever achieves the heightened consciousness of enlightenment (*samadhi*) will find the world transformed into the Kingdom of God. Ramana Marharshi, for example, explains, "The Kingdom of Heaven mentioned in the Bible and this world are not two different regions...The realized being sees this as the Kingdom of Heaven whereas the others see it as 'this world.'" Yogananda concurs, "Heaven is not 'up there,' as people commonly imagine. It is all around us...I see it all the time..." Muktananda adds, "This is the beautiful Garden of Shiva of the Lord, made so that you can walk in it with great joy."

The present-day Hindu yogi Marharishi Mahesh, the founder of the Transcendental Meditation, further claims that his techniques can bring Heaven on Earth to any society.

Buddhism: Buddhist cosmology refers to heavenly realms as the Pure Land. Master Sheng-yen, an enlightened Buddhist monk, asserts that the Pure Land exists here on Earth, though most people cannot see it because of their attachment to self. The popular Buddhist writer Thich Nhat Hanh agrees, stating, "The Pure Land is not somewhere else; it is right here, in the present." And he confides, "There is not one day when I do not walk in the Kingdom of God."

"We are *now* in heaven."
Suzuki (Zen Teacher, Author)

The Tibetan Buddhist teacher Sogyal Rinpoche says, by working directly with our fixed perceptions of the world, seekers find

Heaven on Earth. He explains, "All our old concepts of the world or matter or even ourselves are purified and dissolved, and an entirely new, what you could call 'heavenly' field of vision and perception opens up." Zen masters like Mipham and Yuansou describe the subtle light of this heavenly vision throughout Creation, and Yung-Chia, a Zen master also, adds, "The Gate of Heaven is wide open with not a single obstruction before it."

Islam: Sufism, the mystical branch of Islam, has many famous mystical poets, such as Rumi, Kabir, Hafiz, and Khayyam who describe the intoxicating reality of the imminent divine that blurs all distinctions between this world and the next. For them, Heaven is found in the experience of ecstasy arising with closeness to the divine Presence, which can turn even prison into a "lover's garden." The Muslim scholar Chittick tells us further that the Garden may be entered in experiences of "felicity," the 99 names of God characterizing His qualities and nature, and other achievements of spiritual perfection, such as the complete melting of the ego-self in the Divine Being. Ibn al-'Arabi, a 13th century Islamic scholar and mystical philosopher, adds, "This world is the way to eternal bliss and good, worthy to be cherished and worthy to be praised." Or, in the words of one Sufi saying, "When we stop complaining, we will be in paradise."

I was a Hidden Treasure and I longed to be known, so I created the world so I might be known.
Hadith Qudsi (Islamic Scripture)

Taoism: Taoism speaks of the divine Presence that existed prior to Creation and fulfilled itself in the unfolding of Heaven, Earth and humankind, all of which were at one time unified and undivided. Lao Tzu, the 6th century B.C.E. Chinese sage, calls this Presence the Tao, or "way of life," and taught that sensing the way of Heaven allows men how to live properly and wisely on Earth. Other Taoist teachers, like Takakusu, point to the timeless unity of Heaven and Earth that still exists before mind, desire and preference artificially divide them. The Chinese poet Li Po, describing the timeless mystical beauty all around us, concludes simply, "There is another heaven and earth beyond the world of men."

Existence is beyond the power of words to define... If name be needed, wonder names it all. From wonder into wonder, existence opens.
Lao Tzu (Taoist Sage)

Native Americans: Though Native American beliefs vary some across tribes, they universally espouse a Creation-based spirituality that experiences the world and everything in it as sacred with no history of a "fall" from grace. To Suquamish Chief Seattle, a Puget Sound visionary living in the first half of the 19th century, every "...hillside, every valley, every clearing and wood, is holy..." Donna Ladkin, an expert on Native American spirituality, explains that this experienced holiness implies that the Kingdom of Heaven is here already. Because tribal people see themselves inhabiting a sacred universe, Vine Deloria, a Native American scholar, claims that revelation takes place simply in the adapting to life itself. Explaining that for Native Americans the natural world manifests the divine glory of ultimate reality itself, Catholic monk and mystic Wayne Teasdale concludes simply, "...the earth itself is their church."

Mythology

In his wonderful work on the mythology of Heaven on Earth, "Memories and Visions of Paradise," Richard Heinberg explains that nearly all ancient peoples believed in a time when Heaven and Earth were one and a future time when they would be unified once again. Yet, the ultimate essence and achievement of Paradise, he argues, occurs in mystical experiences, a conclusion supported by the great mythologist Joseph Campbell. John Ashton and Tom Whyte narrate myths from around the world describing adventures to a heavenly destination on Earth in their book, "The Quest for Paradise." Interestingly, such adventures often originate during spiritually-awakened states of consciousness.

Popular culture, too, continues to create myth-like tales of Paradise including Shangri'La, from James Hilton's popular 1933 novel "Lost Horizon," and Brigadoon, from the 1947 musical of the same name by Jay Lerner and Frederick Loewe. In fact, the Weekly World News, a tabloid like the National Inquirer, reported on August 15, 2005 that the military, while searching for weapons of mass destruction in Iraq, had stumbled upon the remains of the original Garden of Eden. More amazingly, the military was now growing a new Tree of Life.

The power of myths even led early theologians and cartographers to place Paradise on world maps — the Chinese located it in central Asia, the Hindus in the Himalayans and the Christian Europeans in the extreme east. Indeed, Columbus actually believed he had discovered Paradise upon first glimpsing the coast of Venezuela in 1498. In his well-researched treatise, "Mapping Paradise," Allesandro Scafi charts this universal idea throughout history, from early Christians to twenty-first century Internet sites, concluding, "There is still no end to the stream of theories on the exact position of the mythical Garden of Eden."

Archeology

Archeologists document a 2000-year period in which the Goddess served as the center of religious life and Earth was still considered – and experienced – as a sacred place. From 6500 to 4500 BC, in an area known as "Old Europe," people lived in a peaceful, matrilineal and agrarian culture that considered the Earth as the actual body of the Goddess. Later patriarchal religions lost this vision by trivializing the Goddess and conceptualizing the cosmos in dualistic categories, such as sacred and profane, spirit and matter and Heaven and Earth. Documenting this transition in their book, "The Myth of the Goddess," Anne Baring and Jules Ashford explain, "The Mother Goddess, wherever she is found, is an image that inspires and focuses a perception of the universe as an organic, alive and sacred whole...the divine was immanent as creation."

Naturalists

Inspired naturalists, too, have seen Heaven on Earth, for they often look so closely at the beauty of the world that they finally see into the underlying splendor of Creation. Wayne Teasdale describes nature as "a revelation of the divine" and comments, "When we are caught up in the breathless immensity of a sunrise or sunset, are we not given a glimpse of a hidden revelation?" It should not surprise us, then that naturalist like John Muir often describe the wilderness with near-religious ecstasy or that Marghanita Laski's research found nature and nature art to be common triggers for mystical experience. For naturalist John Burroughs, one of our most important lessons involves seeing "that heaven lies about us in this world," a sentiment shared by American author Henry David Thoreau who, witnessing an unexpectedly beautiful scene, declared, "Heaven is under our feet as well as over out heads."

Etymology

The experience of Heaven also hides in our everyday vocabulary waiting for us to rediscover what our words secretly imply. For example, definitions for Heaven and Paradise commonly emphasize great beauty, happiness and perfection, and one of the meanings of bliss is heavenly rapture. Such definitions seem to confirm that a subtle awareness of Heaven may slip into consciousness during intense experiences of beauty and joy, hardly surprising since such experiences constitute qualities of Heaven on Earth in the first place.

Poetry

Poets naturally sense the presence of Heaven on Earth. William Wordsworth, recalling his early childhood, wrote "Heaven lies about us in our infancy," Elizabeth Barrett-Browning observed "Earth's crammed with heaven," Emily Dickinson described Eden as "...the old fashioned House we live in everyday" and Sr. Teresa of Lisieux described her closeness to Jesus as "My Heaven on Earth."

Mystical Experiences

Even today, awareness of Heaven on Earth opens to people who find themselves unexpectedly graced with mystical consciousness. Robert Johnson, a popular Jungian author, recalled, "Suddenly I was in a glorious world. It was pure light, gold, radiant, luminous, ecstatically happy, perfectly beautiful, purely tranquil, joy beyond bound...It was all that any mystic ever promised of heaven, and I knew then that I was in possession of the greatest treasure known to humankind."

Katherine Trevelyan, recalling her own profound mystical experience in her autobiography, adds, "The wonder was beyond anything I have ever read or imagined or heard men speak about. I was Adam walking alone in the first Paradise...Every flower spoke to me, every spider wove a miracle of intricacy for my eyes, every bird understood that here was Heaven come to earth...Every prayer was fulfilled, every possible desire for the whole world consummated; for His Kingdom had come and I had beheld it with my very eyes."

Others, like Henry David Thoreau and me, experienced Heaven on Earth in early childhood and subsequently pursued a life long quest for this vision again. In fact, in his lovely collection of childhood mystical experiences, "Visions of Innocence," Edward Hoffman explains, "Most fundamentally, it now appears undeniable that some of us (perhaps far more than we suspect) have undergone tremendous peak – even mystical – experiences during our early years," experiences that induce a "lifelong interest in mystical teachings." Indeed, the psychologist, scholar and philosopher, Jean Houston, reports that people in her workshops often recall memories of Paradise from early childhood. She calls these memories "mythic remembrances of Eden."

Thus, as Evelyn Underhill documented in her classic work, "Mysticism," the world transfigured into Paradise has been witnessed by countless saints and mystics throughout history. Underlining our own responsibility for awakening the experience of Heaven to Earth, Andrew Cohen, mystic and publisher of the spiritual magazine "What Is Enlightenment?" suggests that a "heavenly realm here on earth" is "entirely dependent upon us."

Closely connected with the sense of the 'Presence of God,' or power of perceiving the Absolute, is the complementary mark of the illuminated consciousness; the vision of 'a new heaven and a new earth.'
Evelyn Underhill (Scholar of Mystical)

Ordinary Experiences
Finally, people actually experience Heaven all the time without realizing it. Song lyrics ("I'm in Heaven"), love notes and greeting cards ("You are heavenly"), and exclamations ("Oh my heavens!") all refer to the immediate contact with Paradise that occurs whenever a particularly joyous or heightened emotional state momentarily provides a glimpse and experience of Heaven on Earth. As I described in my book, "Ordinary Enlightenment," moments of heightened perception occur far more often than we realize. Unfortunately, we wrongly attribute these heavenly experiences to temporary emotional conditions – like falling in love or the sharpened sensory perception associated with awe or what we feel when we see a beautiful sunset. Our culture's conviction that Heaven never could exist in a world filled with so

much suffering and evil supports this error. Rumored for thousands of years, Heaven on Earth may actually be but a blink away, as Carol and Philip Zaleski happily point out in their anthology, "The Book of Heaven."

Aging

In his wonderful book, "Still Here," Ram Dass reminds us that the world's great religions always have taught that the doorway to the Kingdom of Heaven is found in the eternal now, an opening he associates with the experience of aging. In "Death of a Hero, Birth of the Soul," I argue that this sense of eternity becomes ever more immediate and real in the aging process, which dissolves the conceptual barriers of identity, time and story. Continuing this theme in "But Where Is God? Psychotherapy and the Religious Search," I hypothesized that the divine Self gradually becomes a new center of consciousness for the enlightened elder, in turn revealing a divine reality inside and out. In her book on aging, Marsha Sinetar affirms the relationship between experiences of Presence and Paradise, suggesting that as we awaken in God's Presence in our later years, we discover that rather than aiming for Paradise, "We are Paradise."

It should be apparent by now that Heaven on Earth does not represent just a romantic fantasy. In light of so many declarations and first-hand descriptions, I find it amazing that so few "modern" people know or write about Heaven on Earth. Hopefully, the information I've provided in this chapter has convinced you that rather than being my own eccentric point of view, Heaven on Earth is, in fact, a universal prophecy and ultimate realization – one that you too can experience.

CHAPTER 4

Heaven's Compass

A map that shows paradise as part of the world involves a leap of the imagination. Mapping paradise is simultaneously a confession of belief in a God who operates within terrestrial space and of the limits of human reasoning.
Alessandro Scafi (Historian)

Where is paradise? Does it have walls? Is there a map to find it? Need one walk through the valleys of torment? Does one have to die physically? I think not...One can be in paradise by simply saying 'yes' to this moment. Regardless of what seems to be taking place in the illusion of your surroundings, when you say yes, you are in loving truth – you are in no-time, you have touched eternity. You are, indeed, in paradise. The mind will still dismiss it as a fairy tale, but the heart knows it is true.
Pat Rodegast (Spiritual Author)

Eventually all who walk the road to higher knowing come to one realization: I had it all the time. Some arrive sooner, and some arrive later; some arrive by the path of pain and others by the way of joy; some come alone and some come together. In the end, the method is not as important as the goal.
Alan Cohen (Spiritual Author)

Introduction
Just as my invisible compass pointed me in the direction of Heaven on Earth, the metaphor of a compass provided me with a way to organize the four realms of spiritual life into a model of our journey to Heaven on Earth. Used as a noun, the word

"compass" means an instrument for determining direction. Indeed, a compass' freely moving needle always points to magnetic north, and establishing one direction permits easy deduction of the other three. Used as a verb, "compass" means to go round, grasp mentally or achieve an end. Thus, Heaven's Compass represents a navigational tool, a method of understanding and a spiral journey toward a goal. Let me show you how to employ Heaven's Compass to describe and map a course to our destination: Heaven on Earth.

Heaven's Compass and the Four Realms of Spiritual Life

The Story of Creation I shared in Chapter 1 revealed four realms of spiritual life: *Divinity*, the infinite consciousness of the Creator; *Heaven on Earth*, the Creator becoming Creation; the *World of Man*, human beliefs superimposed on Creation; and *Darkness*, the psychological space where emotional wounds and the pain of Heaven's loss lie hidden. These four realms make up Heaven's Compass (see Figure 1).

World of Man (Beliefs)	Heaven on Earth (Creation)
Darkness (Unconscious)	Divinity (God)

Heaven's Compass
(Figure 1)

To learn more about each, let's take a tour through the four realms of Heaven's Compass. While the Story of Creation begins with

Divinity, we shall start with the World of Man, for it is here that most of us have lost our way and where most of us must, therefore, begin the journey.

The World of Man

A realm composed of endless concepts, stories and beliefs, the World of Man makes up a vast intellectual lens concealing Heaven on Earth. Its concepts, stories and beliefs tell us who we are, what we should do, think and be, how the world works, and especially what's wrong with our lives. It represents an entirely manmade construction founded largely on patriarchal values, such as hierarchy, control and ownership. It operates through the laws, values and social norms governing our beliefs and behavior.

> *We are what we think. All that we are arises with our*
> *thoughts. With our thoughts we make the world.*
> Buddha (6th Century BCE Chinese Sage)

Among all the ideas in the World of Man, the self-concept (also called the ego, self-image, or persona in the spiritual and psychological literature) creates the most problems. Based on who you – and others – *think* you are, the self-concept generates constant worries. For example, we ask ourselves, "Am I good enough, smart enough, attractive enough, or rich enough?" Then we worry that we aren't – and that other people see us this way as well, and we compare ourselves to others. Indeed, we might just as well call this realm the "land of worried thoughts," because its beliefs stir up enormous amounts of fear, doubt, envy, competition, and self-criticism.

Do you remember the shock you felt the first time you were viewed by others in a highly negative or critical way? My friend Tim does. As a very young child, he recalls being the apple of his mother's eye, so the idea of "being Tim" – his self-concept –

seemed mostly positive. Around the age of five, however, conflict in his parents' marriage began to wear on his mother, and one day, in place of her gentle, attentive response to his bid for attention, she blew up. "Stop bothering me!" she yelled. "It's time for you to grow up. You're too old to act like a baby." Suddenly, Tim realized that his mother had formed the very negative concept of him "acting like a baby" and he feared that this concept might end their loving relationship. Suppressing his need for love, however, left him feeling sad and lonely. To solve this terrible conflict, Tim decided to become a "good boy," a better self-concept that meant exhibiting behavior deserving of love. So, Tim morphed into a serious, "grown up" child. He looked after his mother and little brother, got "A's" on every report card and worried a lot about how others perceived him. In other words, he constantly tried to project a nearly perfect self-concept.

Like Tim, all children sooner or later discover the importance of the self-concept. Success in education, relationships, business, fashion, and social opinion derives from the continued enhancement of one's self-presentation. What we wear, how we behave, what is on our resume, all contribute to our own self-concept as well as to the way the world perceives us.

Though only an idea, we believe the self-concept actually defines us. Just as the word "cat" is not the same as the animal in front of you (the former represents a fixed idea in the mind and the latter a dynamic, living process in the world), the concepts you have about yourself are not the same as you – until you believe them. Put another way, the real you experienced within arises as a natural and spontaneous process, like a flower, utterly separate from any words or ideas you have about it.

If you think you are free, you are free. If you think you are bound, you are bound. For the saying is true: You are what you think.
Ashtavakra Gita (Ancient Hindu Scripture)

In the same way we impose concepts on ourselves – baby, bad boy, not smart enough, no fashion sense, uneducated, we also impose them on others. In other words, we mostly see our ideas, views, or stereotypes of them – an old woman, rude yuppi, homeless person, corrupt politician, bored waitress, cute child, lonely housewife, sexy movie star, dangerous criminal, disabled person, etc. – rather than who they really are.

In addition, in the same way that we categorize people based on our ideas about them, we also fail to see Heaven on Earth. Instead of seeing the true essence of things, we view them through the lenses of the World of Man's shared conceptual vocabulary: city, streets, houses, offices, stores, restaurants, farms, mountains, rivers, and clouds. Favoring the mind's ideas, concepts, and beliefs over pure perception, we lose sight of Creation and live in the virtual reality of the mind.

The beliefs that dominate the World of Man stir up all the confusion, unhappiness, greed, conflict, and warfare that fill this world. Like a soap opera, this realm thrives on high drama: romantic fantasies, heroic quests, political power struggles, the conflict of good versus evil, and our struggles to survive, to be good enough and to find love. And just like a T.V. show, all this exists entirely as mental fantasies. As those fantasies play in our minds, they conceal the divine world all around us.

I think therefore I am.
Descartes (17th Century French Philosopher)

I don't mean to devalue conceptual thought as inherently bad or wrong. Quite the contrary, it represents the divine gift behind countless wonderful creations – science, medicine, law, engineering, technology, religion, and literature. Indeed, the whole organization of society and civilization depends upon the ordering principles of thought. For example, clocks, calendars, maps, laws, books, roles, values, and professions all require conceptual thought. Beliefs in the World of Man become a source of problems, however, when we regard them as the true and only correct perception of reality, such as when collective stereotypes lead to prejudice and war, when our negative self-concepts trigger depression or when rigid beliefs about reality prevent our seeing Heaven on Earth all around us.

Exercise

Because we live in the World of Man so much of the time, we assume we know it well. We do, but that's also the problem. We know it too well. In fact, we have become so completely absorbed in our beliefs and fantasies that we unquestionably consider them true.

To begin understanding what fills your conceptual world, let's explore the common thoughts and fantasies in your inner life. Take a few minutes to answer the question: Who am I? List all the roles and beliefs that seem to make you what you are. Next list the five things you worry about most. Then list and describe your three most frequent fantasies.

What did you discover from this exercise? Answer the following questions and see what you learn:

- Do you notice how complex and convincing your self-concept has become and how much thought and imagination revolve around this story of you?
- Do you see how attached you are to these thoughts and fantasies and how much time you spend thinking about them?
- Can you see how concerned you are about the worth of your self-concept compared to the self-concepts of others in your family, school, neighborhood, workplace, or society, and how determined you are to improve it?
- What if people no longer saw you in the favorable light you try to project? How would you feel?

Remember, your self-concept consists of a made up narrative that exists in the mind only. It is not you unless you believe it. Finally, realize that this inner world of thought and fantasy constantly separates you from Heaven on Earth.

Tim spent 45 years trying to be good enough to deserve others' love and approval. He became very good at what he did, reached the top of his profession and now seems to be the perfect father and husband. On the outside, he has his act together, but it is only an act. The self-concept of goodness now controls Tim and keeps him imprisoned in the World of Man.

Darkness

As light symbolizes consciousness and knowledge, so Darkness symbolizes their absence. Our language readily captures this understanding with phrases like "shedding light on a subject" or "being in the dark." The realm of Darkness, therefore, comprises unconsciousness and all that we do not know. This realm seems dark when we are in it. It also feels scary and sad, and like a place where we cannot see well enough to find the path back to the light.

Interestingly, a subtle relationship often exists between the thoughts, ideas and concepts of the World of Man and Darkness. Thought actually can short-circuit consciousness and knowledge. For example, when we label something ("It's a bird.") and thereafter ignore all its qualities (color, song, diet, mating behavior, life cycle, and migratory patterns), such knowledge gets excluded from our consciousness. We remain "in the dark" about it. We overlook most of Creation in this way. For instance, we see a sunset, and, rather than really taking in its glorious palette of subtly evolving colors, we say, "Oh that's pretty," and go inside.

If you bring forth what is within you, what you bring forth will save you. If you do not bring forth what is within you, what you do not bring forth will destroy you.
Jesus (Founder of Christianity)

This process also overrides our perception of emotions, for we can literally talk ourselves out of what we feel and temporarily replace those emotions with what we think we feel. For example, you can talk yourself into liking or trusting someone when, deep down, you really don't, or you can think happy thoughts to suppress the sadness you feel. Darkness becomes the unconsciousness described by psychologists when we hide our feelings and perceptions so well we can't remember them.

In much the same way, we also find ourselves in Darkness when we allow others' concepts and ideas about who we should be to govern who we are. For example, Susan grew up in a very strict household with no television, dancing or sleep-overs. Church, school and chores made up her life. So much of who she was born to be – outgoing, fun loving and adventurous – didn't fit her parents' model of a proper young lady. After years of being called rebellious, strong-willed and even sinful, Susan gave up and forced herself to become the paragon of virtue others wanted. She constructed a life of piety, duty and devotion. Only her chronic, low-grade depression and inability to feel happiness belied this facade. Because most of her true self – who she was born to be – felt unwanted, Susan hurt on the inside all the time. Rather than bringing forth her divinely given gift of self, she hid it away, and the grief caused by this self-betrayal pulled her down into depression and into Darkness.

In darkness and nothingness, in the silence and emptying, in the letting go and letting be, and in the pain and suffering that constitute an equally real part of our spiritual journey.
Mathew Fox (Theologian, Author)

Valuing only the thoughts and beliefs prized by the World of Man means keeping much of what we feel and see – including who we really are – hidden in the Darkness within. As a result, Darkness also could be called the "land of pain and betrayal," because it hurts so much when we – or others – criticize or reject the precious gift of self.

Susan's self-betrayal eventually broke her heart. When she began crying uncontrollably "for no reason" and expressed a desire to die, she began psychotherapy sessions. In time, her therapist helped her re-evaluate – and revalue – her discarded self, and Susan begin to bring forth what was inside — a wonderful, outgoing nature, and she did so with no guilt or apologies. As the saying goes, "Who you are is God's gift to you. What you do with it is your gift to God." Combining her love for people, fun and adventure, Susan became an inner-city school-teacher specializing in student field trips all over the country. Now she felt happy, alive and truly useful. Light had been brought into her Darkness.

When I speak of darkness, I am referring to a lack of knowing. It is a lack of knowing that includes everything you do not know or else that you have forgotten....And for this reason it is called...a cloud of unknowing that is between you and your God.
The Cloud of Unknowing (Anonymous 14th Century English Mystic)

The final aspect of Darkness, described by an anonymous 14th century English mystic as a "Cloud of Unknowing," consists of a mental space completely empty of thought, beliefs, ideas, knowledge, plans, identity, goals, or even hope. As we will see, Heaven's Compass suggests that we must pass through this ultimate void to experience that which lies beyond thought: Divinity and Heaven on Earth. T.S. Elliot describes this passage beautifully in his poem East Coker:

I said to my soul, be still, and let the dark come upon you Which shall be the darkness of God...

I said to my soul, be still, and wait without hope
For hope would be hope of the wrong thing; wait without love
For love would be love of the wrong thing; there is yet faith,
But the faith and love and the hope are all in the waiting.
Wait without thought, for you are not ready for thought:
So the darkness shall be the light, and the stillness the dancing...
The laughter in the garden, echoed ecstasy
Not lost, but requiring, pointing to the agony
Of death and birth.

The light of Divinity and the ecstasy of its garden shine on the other side of Darkness, but to reach these realms requires dying to who we think we are in the World of Man. In that dying process, which takes place in Darkness, everything we think we are must dissolve along with thinking itself. For example, following my anesthesia awareness experience, I had to release my World of Man identity as a psychologist and pass through an inner Darkness filled with grief and unknowing in order to continue the journey to Heaven on Earth. Susan, too, gave up her World of Man identity as a rebellious and strong-willed sinner to travel through the dark underworld, find her real self and give birth to a new life. From this archetypal passage of death and rebirth, we find ourselves renewed in the innocence and purity of Heaven on Earth – until we fall back again into narrow and controlling ideas of self and world.

Exercise
What lies buried in your realm of Darkness? Consider these possibilities and circle one:

- Unacceptable feelings about your present life
- Parts of your true self that were rejected long ago
- Emotional wounds that you never healed
- Forgotten memories of Heaven on Earth

- The capacity for joy and ecstasy

Now reflect on the item you chose, and answer these questions:

- Why have you kept this material hidden?
- What has been the cost of hiding it?
- How has suppressing this material kept you locked in the Darkness?
- What would you have to feel or experience if you got in touch with this material?
- What might you gain by letting this material into consciousness?
- How has suppressing this material blocked your journey to Heaven on Earth?

Everyone hides a realm of Darkness within. Entering it requires recognizing Darkness exists and facing what may lie hidden within it. In addition, entering it requires motivation – realizing the journey inward is both necessary and valuable, sensitivity – to really get in touch with the memories and emotions hidden there, courage – to face painful feelings and memories, kindness – to love and accept what we find without judgment, patience – to process the hurt in its own timing which may seem slow and frustrating, and forgiveness – of ourselves and others for the events that created the Darkness. Sometimes, too, we may need the help or guidance of friends, family, therapists, or clergy to avoid getting stuck in depression, bitterness, or unresolved issues. Know that the relief of pain and suffering, and the renewal of our movement into the sacred, make this journey through Darkness worth the emotional cost.

It took three painful years of therapy for me to heal the devastated 14-year-old boy found in the Darkness of anesthesia and three more years of spiritual education to reconnect with my soul and its vision. Your journey through Darkness may take a completely different form and course, for each person's experience follows a pattern as unique as their fingerprint. Yet, the archetypal "agony of death and birth" composes the common narrative underlying every great descent into Darkness and represents its secret meaning, purpose and value.

Divinity

Our tour through Heaven's Compass now moves into Divinity, the source and consciousness of Creation. The mystics tell us the Universe is conscious and alive; everywhere and everything is saturated with a divine Presence. Called by countless names – God, Yahweh, Great Spirit, Allah, Jesus, Buddha, Emptiness, Brahman, Creator, Goddess, Holy Ghost, Shechinah, Tao, Jehovah, Cosmic Consciousness, the Force – this infinite and sacred consciousness permeates Creation and serves as the intelligence, creativity and love responsible for all existence and life itself. We reach the realm of Divinity through the experience of Presence.

The material world is nothing but Consciousness. Space, time, matter, energy, life, mind – all that we encounter and experience – are forms of Consciousness. It is all one Consciousness.
Shraddhananda (Swami, Author)

Though it may sound simplistic, we actually locate the Presence by sensing pure consciousness. As I described in Chapter 2, the experience of Divinity lies beyond ideas and beliefs. Sensing the Presence, therefore, involves focusing intentionally heightened and thoughtless consciousness back on itself. Experiencing consciousness within – silent and still – brings us into Divinity's Presence inside ourselves. Learning to heighten and focus awareness around us, we find Presence extending everywhere as space itself – conscious, alive and aware. Like Heaven on Earth, Presence never left this earthly plane or left us, rather we left it. This understanding of Presence seems simplistic because cultural fantasies of meeting God, such as trumpets sounding or seeing a shining old man dressed in white standing on a cloud, cause us to ignore the imminence of Divinity right here, right now.

This universe is a single living being embracing all living beings within it, and possessing a single Soul that permeates all its parts to the degree of their participation in it.
Plotinus (3rd Century Egyptian Philosopher)

As we learn to sense the Presence ever more fully, we discover a timeless consciousness filled with peace, tenderness and love. This realm could also be called the "land of pure joy," because of the feelings it evokes. Time spent in the Presence dissolves worried thoughts and fantasies, as well as the problems they create. Melting into the Divine, we take on its generous, silent, and infinitely loving nature, and all we do flows from this greater Self – our truest nature, the divine consciousness secreted inside our own consciousness.

People temporarily experience Divinity through spiritual practices, spontaneous mystical experiences, the "zone" of athletic competition, and the development of mystical consciousness. However, most of us experience Divinity partially and transiently. For those who learn the art of mystical consciousness described in Chapter 6, Divinity becomes an increasingly common center of awareness influencing all we feel, think and do.

Exercise
Ask yourself, "When have I felt especially close to the Presence?" It might have been in church, in the wilderness, alone or with others, during a crisis, or on a retreat. This event doesn't have to

be a big mystical experience. In fact, you may not have realized that you felt the Presence until later. Continue to dwell on this question until a specific memory comes into mind, and then answer these questions in enough detail to bring back the actual experience:

- Where and when did this experience happen?
- What exactly took place?
- How did it feel?
- Did your perception of others or the world change during the experience?
- How were you affected afterwards?
- How does it feel to recall this event now?

God is as pervasive and perceptible as the atmosphere in which we are bathed. He encompasses us on all sides, like the world itself.
Teilhard de Chardin (Jesuit Priest, Paleontologist, Philosopher)

Humanistic psychologist Abraham Maslow studied mystical experiences and discovered nearly every one he interviewed could recall such first-hand awareness of the sacred, though they may have forgotten or mislabeled it. This exercise helps you rediscover your mystical experiences and see what else they may have to teach you. Unlike common memories, mystical experiences also tend to hold their original vividness and significance, so that in recalling them new meanings and realizations emerge. Another interesting feature of these experiences comes when people share their memories with each other. Not only does the listener often realize new features of their own experiences, a sense of holiness begins to expand into the room and touches everyone. In these ways, mystical memories not only teach us about the sacred, they actually seem to awaken the experience of God's Presence again.

Heaven on Earth

In the awakened consciousness of Presence, Divinity shines as the world itself. We see Divinity as everything around us. Our reality is cleansed, renewed and transfigured into Heaven on Earth. This realm may be called Creation when referring to the Biblical Garden of Eden or our original experiences of the divine world in early childhood. It also could be called the "land of wonder and love," because of its astonishing beauty, perfection and holiness.

"Where shall I look for Enlightenment?" the disciple asked.
"Here," the elder said.
"When will it happen? the disciple asked.
"It's happening right now," the elder answered.
"Then why don't I experience it?" the disciple persisted.
"Because you do not look," the elder said.
Joan Chittister (Benedictine Sister, Author)

One person described this realm by saying, "For the first time in my life I caught a glimpse of the ecstatic beauty of reality...I saw no new thing, but I saw all the usual things in a miraculous new light – in what I believe is their true light...I saw how wildly beautiful and joyous, beyond any words of mine to describe, is the whole of life...My heart melted out of me in a rapture of love and delight."

Another individual observed, "I felt that the world of nature was utterly right and literally an act of God's, and that to know this, and to be permitted to appreciate so much of the wonderful and the adorable, was nothing less than bliss. And this was reality. That is the whole point."

Yet another person, "We dwell in a fairyland of unimaginable beauty and sublimity and know nothing of it."

These people were equally certain that during the course of their experiences the world had become divine. One person explained, "Everything was alive and God was present in all things; in fact the earth, all plants and animals and people seemed to be made of God." Another individual recalled, "A voice whispered in my soul: God is all. He is not far away in the heaven; He is here. This grass under your feet is He; this bountiful harvest, that blue sky, those roses in your hand – you yourself are all one with Him."

Many people resist viewing this world as Heaven on Earth. They ask, "What about all the terrible things going on, like illness, poverty and war? To find Heaven, we must understand that we create the ugliness around us with our stories, beliefs and actions. We see what we think and imagine, projecting our ideas and fantasies onto the world like a movie, and then we react to this movie in ways that cause more suffering, injustice, hatred, and violence. For example, seeing "terrorists" instead of wounded, suffering and humiliated people, we tell stories encouraging violence over reconciliation. The radiant divine world lies hidden beneath these stories waiting for us to wake up from our collective nightmare and see it.

Creation is the extension of God.
Creation is God encountered in time and space.
Creation is the infinite in the garb of the finite.
To attend to creation is to attend to God
To attend to the moment is to attend to eternity.
To attend to the part is to attend to the whole.
To attend to Reality is to live constructively.
Pirke Avot (The Talmud)

Exercise

As Joan Chittister and Evelyn Underhill suggest in the earlier quotes, transforming our perception of the world begins when we look at something with a heightened, undivided and thoughtless awareness in the immediate here and now. This cleansing of consciousness allows us to see the world without the filter of thought, names and expectations.

To start seeing Divinity and the divine world, try this simple exercise: Look intensely at something in your surroundings, but do so as if you were seeing it for the very first time — without words, thoughts or expectations. Heighten your sensory perception – see, hear, touch, smell, even taste the object – to experience the thing exactly as it is – radically new, fresh, richly detailed, captivating. Create a timeless consciousness, unencumbered by concerns about past, present and future. Just stay present in the moment. Then, take a few minutes to write down what you experienced.

All that is asked is that we shall look for a little time, in a special and undivided manner, at some simple, concrete, and external thing. This object of our contemplation may be almost anything we please... Do not think... Almost at once, this new method of perception will reveal unsuspected qualities in the external world... Seen thus, a thistle has celestial qualities: a speckled hen a touch of the sublime.
Evelyn Underhill (Scholar of Mysticism)

Following these instructions, you'll discover the world is not what you think. This place, intensely examined with a consciousness free of thought, becomes brighter, clearer, more colorful, and more beautiful than anything you could imagine. If you continue practicing this exercise, soon you may even begin to feel the simple, absolute joy of existence. If so, you have reached the threshold of Heaven on Earth. Keep in mind, however, that this exercise awakens only a small or "threshold" experience of Heaven on Earth. The ultimate transformation takes place in God's Presence (described in Chapters 6 and 7). For the time being, keep practicing these basic perceptual skills as preparation for crossing the threshold and actually entering Heaven on Earth.

CHAPTER 5

The Cycle of Spiritual Experience

*To everything there is a season, a time for every purpose under
the sun.*
Bible: "Ecclesiastes"

*All insight, all revelation, all illumination, all love, all that is genuine,
all that is real, lies in now – and in the attempt to create now we
approach the inner precincts, the holiest part of life. For in time all
things are seeking completion, but in now all things are complete.*
Maurice Nicoll (Jungian Analyst, Author)

*The old must often try to be silent, if it is within their power, since
silence may be like space, the intensely alive something that
contains all.*
Florida Scott Maxwell (Jungian Analyst, Author)

Heaven's Compass includes one more important dimension: the
Cycle of Spiritual Experience. This cycle operates all the time in
countless circumstances. Thus, examining its operation greatly
increases our understanding of the appearance and disappearance
of Heaven on Earth in our daily lives. Plus, learning this cycle
allows us to use Heaven's Compass to reach Heaven on Earth.

The Cycle of Spiritual Experience has four stages: betrayal,
descent, reunion, and renewal (ascent). To help you recognize this
sequence, imagine the following vignette:

The Scene: Heaven on Earth
*Picture yourself on a quiet Sunday afternoon busy doing something
you really love, such as reading, painting or gardening, with no*

responsibilities, deadlines, problems, or social expectations impinging on this happy and carefree activity. Imagine how much you enjoy this activity, how your soul sings and how the day feels timeless, precious and "just perfect." Life is beautiful!

We usually become aware of Heaven on Earth when beauty, relaxation and the joy of "just being" dissolve the World of Man to reveal the presence of Heaven on Earth all around us. Expressing natural interests and creativity in a peaceful context liberates the true self – the psychological embodiment of your soul, and you feel its timeless joy. We routinely mislabel this experience of the divine world, calling it "just" a beautiful day or good mood. If we knew how to look, however, we would see so much more. We would see that this is Heaven on Earth.

An anthropologist from another galaxy studying the ways of earthlings would probably look at our habit of warfare, our propensity to chronic anxiety and worry, our tendency to be motivated by guilt and shame, our obsession with work, our creating of stress and psychosomatic illness, and conclude that the human race has a love affair with pain. It is a rare person who is able to tolerate three uninterrupted days of happiness! We are most deeply threatened not by the fires of hell, but by the pleasures of paradise.
Sam Keen (Author)

Betrayal: Stepping into the World of Man

Imagine now that an unwelcome phone call from a co-worker, relative or neighbor suddenly interrupts your free and blissful consciousness. You force yourself to take the call, which ends up lasting more than an hour, while you try to act interested and polite even though you'd rather return to what you were doing. Abandoning your true self and its joy, you put on the "good" false self and suppress feelings of resentment, disappointment or sadness. Perhaps you even fool yourself with this social charade and begin to feel kind of charged up. You may even believe you are having a "good talk" and feel satisfied or smug. You are now well into the World of Man.

Sooner or later, often with a single thought, word or decision, we betray our connection to true self and to Heaven on Earth and create (or return to) the World of Man. The more energy we put into this "good" self-concept, that is, into being someone we think we should be, the more we become trapped in the World of Man's maze of obligations, beliefs, goals, and conventions. We even can convince ourselves that this version of the World of Man provides a rewarding way of life, but this self-deception won't last. Having betrayed the true self, we inflict a wound inside whose knotted and contracted pain now blocks the natural flow of our being.

The fact is that the mad rush of the past 100 years has left us out of breath... We know that the automated machine is here to liberate us and show us the way back to Eden... But we do not know that we have arrived. We stand there panting, caked with sweat and dust afraid to realize that the seventh day of the second creation is here and the ultimate Sabbath is spread out before us.
Eric Hoffer (Social Philosopher)

Descent: Dropping into Darkness

Imagine the phone call finally ending, and as you put down the phone you try to remember what you were doing before the phone rang. Although you can recall your earlier pleasurable activity, the good feeling has vanished. Instead you feel restless, irritable, and slightly depressed. Nothing seems to really interest you. For a while, you suppress this pain and frustration with busy work – cleaning the messy kitchen, but that only makes you madder, because it wasn't your mess, so you discharge your anger at others with nasty and sarcastic comments. Of course, this outlet only generates more pain and negativity around you, and your unhappiness deepens. Finally, you just begin to feel the underlying hurt and disappointment about how this day unfolded. Perhaps you even let yourself cry. Gradually you notice that the hurt seems to be diminishing, especially if you are understanding and forgiving with yourself.

We can stay in the World of Man for a long time, convincing ourselves of the value of being "good" or "productive" people. Sometimes we stay because we enjoy the narcissistic pleasure of appearing wise, successful, important, or popular. However, because all these reasons to stay represent a betrayal of our true self and the joy of Heaven on Earth, this pretense eventually crumbles into the pain we've hidden in the inner Darkness. To heal this wounded self, we must find it, experience it, care for it, and welcome it back into our consciousness. Pain heals when you feel it.

Reunion: Dissolving into the Presence

Now, see yourself resting quietly in the stillness and silence that naturally follow the release of pent up emotions, such as after a good cry, and drift effortlessly into a peaceful, timeless space, free of thought, struggle or goals. Notice how good it feels to just sit there with nothing to do and no one to be, and how you are resting in – and dissolving into – the Presence. With no self-concept or willful effort, your physical being simply relaxes into a reunion with the Divine.

After a healing descent into Darkness, something very subtle happens that most people rarely notice or name. Awareness empties of thought, identity and reactive emotions, and for a few moments we naturally and effortlessly slip into the pure, timeless, uncluttered consciousness that is Divinity. This, of course, happens without thought, for conceptualization would begin to separate us from Divinity again. Like a salt statue dissolving in water, the self-concept dissolves into the omnipresent Divine. We come to rest in the Presence that always has awaited us, always been with us. Here spiritual healing takes place naturally without effort, intention or goal.

In those hushed silent times when the mind becomes still, the body relaxes into infinity, the senses expand to become one with the world – in those glistening times, a subtle luminosity, a serene radiance, a brilliantly transparent clarity shimmers as the true nature of all manifestation.
Ken Wilber (Spiritual Philosopher)

Renewal (Ascent): Return to Heaven on Earth

As you sit in this deep quiet, imagine waiting patiently for new inspiration or desire. Then, suddenly, you know just what you want to do, what would feel really good. Perhaps you feel like resuming your original activity with revived interest or pursuing something altogether new. As you begin, notice how motivation and joy return as inspiration from the true self once again flows into consciousness. As you focus on what you are doing, any thoughts that have arisen naturally disappear, and you are able to become one with the deeply satisfying flow of your activity, which naturally moves you. Experience again the simple beauty and joy of being.

In the deep peace and stillness of this unspoken reunion with the Presence, soul energies of the true self flow back into awareness. We are, in religious language, "born again." Feeling moved by something in our deepest being, inspiration comes alive. With the lens of perception momentarily wiped clean of thought, identity and emotion, existence once again appears incredibly beautiful as its true splendor is revealed. We have returned to the joy and magic of the divine world, at least for a moment, and have completed the cycle through Heaven's Compass.

To surrender to things as they are, in their isness, is to love them as they are; to love them as they are is to be at one with them... By becoming awakened to the isness of creation, we find ourselves in Nirvana – or Heaven – fulfilled to running over , and wonderfully in accord with all beings – human, animal or mere substance.

Ann Bancroft (Professor of Religion, Author)

The following diagram (Figure 2) summarizes the Cycle of Spiritual Experience. The arrows illustrate our continuous counter clockwise movement through the realms of Heaven's Compass.

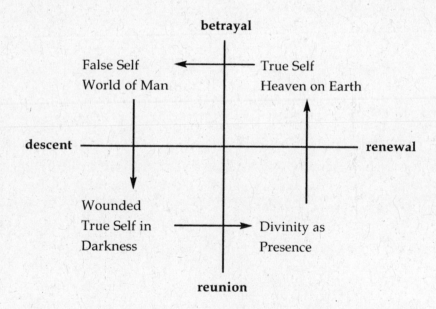

The Cycle of Spiritual Experience (Figure 2)

Exercise

The following study questions will help you see how the Cycle of Spiritual Experience operates in your own life. Take all the time you need to reflect on them, and consider writing your responses in a journal. The more personally and completely you can answer these questions, the greater will be your capacity to see how and why Heaven on Earth moves in and out of your awareness.

- When have you felt close to Heaven on Earth? At the time, what did the world look like and how did it make you feel?
- How do beliefs, rules, and obligations structure your World of Man? What kind of false self-concept have you created there? What parts of the true self have you given up to create this false self?
- Can you feel the pain of your wounded or neglected self buried in the Darkness? How would you describe it? What does this deeper self want?
- Where do you experience the Presence in your everyday life? How does it affect you? How do you tune out the Presence when you're in the World of Man?
- What parts of Heaven on Earth are you giving up in your present life?

Other Cycles of Spiritual Experience

The Cycle of Spiritual Experience operates in all facets of life. Let's consider its circular movement in the areas of relationships, work and the seasons of spiritual life.

Relationships: As poets and songwriters rightly tell us, falling in love, with all the attendant pleasures of lovemaking, can open the gates of Heaven on Earth. The intense, undivided and unconditional love we focus on our beloved reveals their actual Divinity (No wonder our beloved seems perfect and beautiful), and this heightened awareness restores the world's beauty and perfection no matter what else is happening around us. Falling in love returns us to the Garden.

Unfortunately, the standards, values and expectations each partner has internalized from the World of Man begin to encroach upon Paradise. When our lover doesn't live up to our idealized romantic expectations, we become critical and judgmental, and soon conflicts ensue. If the relationship becomes too painful, one or both people consider ending it. Terminating the relationship, however, means starting the cycle over with someone new. Often, addicted to the falling-in-love phase, we do so, as if trying to capture and control the joy of Heaven on Earth through a continual process of falling in love.

Other couples, facing the pain of losing the other, allow love and longing to motivate change and growth. Opening to the Darkness, they gradually face and work through the childhood wounds responsible for their unrealistic idealizations. If your father was abusive, for example, you may seek someone who is quiet and unemotional, and become upset when he displays normal anger. To resolve both the old issues with your father and the current issues with your partner, you will need to heal your hurt around your father's abusive behavior. Relationship conflicts actually serve the purpose of exposing emotional issues that need to be healed for the true self to move out of Darkness.

The wisest couples also learn that all love actually flows from Divinity. When I have loved truly and deeply, I have dissolved into the Presence and its love – indeed I have become the Presence. To experience Divinity in this way heals the relationship and contributes to the revelation of Heaven on Earth. The Cycle of Spiritual Experience teaches us to see our relationships as an opportunity for spiritual work and practice.

Work: Anytime we do the work of our soul – work that expresses our deepest values and gifts, we spend time in Heaven on Earth. This kind of work comes naturally, filled with creativity, generosity, happiness, and love, and it contributes to the building of Heaven on Earth. You don't have to force this work, you do this work because you love it.

When we force ourselves to surrender or compromise the

work of our soul, we step into the World of Man and violate our very nature. If we do this for long, we may even forget what comprises the work of our soul and cynically believe that all work amounts to drudgery, hardship and suffering. I believed, for example, that the responsibility of generating income completely trumped my need for self-expression and, therefore, put off my love of writing (the work of my soul) for decades.

To recover the work of the soul, we must examine our views of work and find out how they formed and caused us to banish our true self to the Darkness. We must also explore how our true nature embodies Divinity and how its gifts contribute to the unfolding beauty of Creation. Time spent in the Presence activates this discovery process, filling the experience of personal presence with the energies and strivings of the Divine. It also awakens our capacity to see and participate in Heaven on Earth.

The Seasons of Spiritual Life: The Cycle of Spiritual Experience creates a much larger pattern expressed in the seasons of spiritual life. Each season has its own meaning, challenges and tasks, and each reflects a part of the journey away from and then back to Heaven on Earth. This journey generates three mega-cycles around Heaven's Compass.

We begin the first cycle in the springtime of life – birth to early adulthood, during which we awaken in Heaven on Earth as Creation but soon surrender it to the World of Man. We pursue this second realm's goals through the long summer of life – early to middle adulthood. By midlife, however, we begin to question the whole concept of identity, achievement and acquisition. The midlife crisis helps us dismantle the false self-concept and descend into the Darkness to recover the true self we experienced in early spring. In the quiet depth within, the Presence rewards us with new possibilities for the self.

The goal of the second of half of life is not private wealth, but the illumination of mankind.
Allan Chinen (Jungian Analyst, Author)

In the fall season of life – post-midlife to old age, we do the work of our soul, initiating a second cycle through Heaven's Compass. Harvesting the essence of our soul, our work is fruitful and rich. Everything we were born to do finds expression, and our life and experiences feel more and more like Heaven on Earth. Eventually the second cycle moves into the winter of life – old age, where the process of aging asks us to surrender both personal identity and the World of Man we internalized as children. Identity fades with the ending of career, family and community roles, and the world we grew up in – its way of life and values – is replaced with one created by younger generations. This second great descent into Darkness asks us to grieve these losses to make room for the Presence to transform us into spiritual elders, so we might see and serve Heaven on Earth. Though few currently understand or pursue this second passage through Darkness and Divinity, humanity's greatest spiritual teachers have outlined its transformational goal: the integration of the divine Self into the personal self and the transfiguration of the Earth. In this mystical round of the cycle, elders increasingly function as wisdom figures and mystics working for the transformation of society and consciousness.

In the third great cycle, the body itself disintegrates into the dark passage of death so we may move through the light into a new kind of cycle in Heaven.

Chapter 5 completes the conceptual preparation for *Finding Heaven Here*. You now understand how humanity lost Creation, the pilgrimage I took to discover it again and the mystics' promise that you, too, can find Heaven on Earth. You also understand Heaven's Compass – our map of the four realms of spiritual life and guide back to Heaven on Earth. We move now into the experiential portion of this book where you will learn to use Heaven's Compass to understand your own spiritual cycles and issues, cleanse your consciousness and finally step across the threshold into Heaven on Earth.

CHAPTER 6

Presence

This 'sense of God' is not a metaphor. Innumerable declarations prove it to be a consciousness as sharp as that which other men have, or think they have, of color, heat, or light.
Evelyn Underhill (Scholar of Mysticism)

We are not seeking to reach God, but rather to achieve a state of stillness so that the awareness of God's presence permeates us.
Joel Goldsmith (Author)

Whether God is transcendent or immanent does not depend on Him, it depends on man.
Martin Buber (Jewish Theologian)

The experience of God's Presence represents the single-most important and powerful force in Heaven's Compass and your first step into Heaven on Earth. As the ultimate source of healing and transformation, you need to experience it directly and intentionally. Therefore, this chapter revolves around a single, powerful exercise, called "Experiencing the Presence," that brings you into the mystical consciousness of Presence, opens a dialogue with God and then returns you to everyday consciousness.

Preparation
Many ways to come into the Presence exist. This exercise serves as just one of them, and I am not claiming that it is better or worse than any other way. However, I teach this exercise because it possesses an unusual power to bring people directly in touch

with the Presence. Please don't confuse Experiencing the Presence with meditation, visualization, guided imagery, or relaxation. This exercise may be different from other practices you've done before.

You may already know how to come into the Presence in your own manner, and that's great. I urge you, however, for the purposes of this book to try this exercise. Later, when you have finished the book, by all means go back to using your current methodology if you feel it works better for you.

Experiencing the Presence guides you through a series of consciousness-transforming "Keys" that we will use over and over again in later chapters. I call them keys, because used correctly they will eventually unlock for you the perceptual gates to the garden of mystical consciousness — Heaven on Earth. For now, don't get concerned about memorizing the Keys or doing them perfectly. In actuality, people have been doing this exercise naturally and without instruction since the dawn of time. You may just need to sharpen your skills.

Before we begin, you'll need to do or remember the following things:

- First, pick a time and place free of interruptions. Give yourself at least an hour to complete the experience, and have paper and pencil handy nearby.
- Second, remember that each Key represents an experiment in consciousness. Thus, try to focus on what does happen, not what doesn't, and see how your experience changes.
- Third, stay positive, and remember that each time you use these Keys, your skill in sensing the Presence will increase.
- Fourth, don't slip back into familiar spiritual routines or practices, because you may end up doing them instead of this exercise.
- Fifth, try not to analyze or figure out what's happening as you practice this exercise. The goal is to stop thinking, not

to generate more thinking.

- Finally, take a moment before you begin to silently ask the Divine to reveal its Presence to you in some way during this exercise, and then notice and trust what takes place.

God is the most obvious thing in the world. He is absolutely self-evident – the simplist and closest reality of life and consciousness. We are only unaware of him because we are too complicated, for our vision is darkened by the complexity of pride... all the time we are unaware of the truth that 'God is nearer to us then we are to ourselves.'
Alan Watts (Author)

Exercise: Experiencing the Presence

Begin by becoming quiet and still for a few moments. You may wish to light a candle or say a prayer to focus your awareness on the sacred. Now pull your awareness away from the outer world of people and events and into your own personal space, that is, into your body and the 6 to 12 inches around your body. Quietly feel your body's energy and sensations for a few moments, noticing the natural rhythm of your breathing at the same time.

The first Key is to *Stop Thinking*. You already know how to do this. You've done it countless times before, maybe when you thread a needle, arrange flowers or paint trim, when your thoughts become suspended for a moment while you complete what you are doing. Notice, too, that all these activities involve a shift into sensory awareness as you move from conception to perception. For example, when I look out the window and visually scan the mountain in the distance, carefully examining the contours of individual trees against the sky, my thinking stops by itself and remains silent as long as I remain in this visual mode. In this way, sensation actually arrests thought. So "come to your senses," and every time you find yourself back in thought, silently repeat the Key, "Stop Thinking," as a reminder to return to sensory awareness. Practice this first Key for a few moments until it describes your present state of awareness – in other words, until your mind is devoid of thought.

> *The holy time is quiet as a nun, breathless with adoration... Listen! The mighty being is awake.*
> William Wordsworth (English Poet)

The second Key is to *"Intensify Awareness and Perception in the Present."* In other words, heighten your awareness. Wake up! Be as conscious and alert as you can. Pretend that your life depends in this moment on being wide awake and totally present. Now practice these first two Keys for a few moments until they describe your present state of awareness – super aware and conscious but with your mind free of thoughts.

The third Key directs you to focus this thought-free heightened awareness on the world around you. It asks you to *"Experience the World Exactly As It Is,"* as if you've never seen it so clearly before. Look intensely at your hands, the fabric of your clothes, your chair, or something nearby. Bring your vision into extremely sharp focus as if you are adjusting a microscope until you suddenly see things incredibly clearly. Use your other senses as well: Smell the room, listen to the sounds around you, feel the remarkable sensitivity in your fingertips. Notice how amazing things really are when you stop to experience them directly with intense sensory perception. Now practice the first three Keys for a few moments until they describe your present state of awareness – super aware and conscious, experiencing the world around you clearly with new eyes and with all your senses but with a mind free of thoughts.

Let's go even further into mystical consciousness. The fourth Key is to *"Come Into The Presence Through Your Own Presence,"* that is, through pure consciousness. While still focusing on a specific perception (for example, your hand or clothing), tune into your own presence, that is, the experience of your own consciousness. In other words, become conscious of consciousness itself, aware of the experience of awareness. Put another way, you already know how to focus on thoughts or sensations, this Key asks you to focus on the consciousness in which they arise, a space which may be sensed as emptiness or silence. Sense this empty consciousness as clearly and distinctly as you can.

Presence is the most fundamental, although usually subliminal, experience of reality...It is omnipresent.
Ralph Harper (Professor of Humanities)

Then, in this wide-awake stillness, see if you can notice one more amazing thing: Notice that consciousness exists everywhere. It is not in you; you are in it. Sense space itself as conscious, aware and alive. You have arrived in the Presence. Now practice the first four Keys for a few moments until they describe your present state of awareness – super aware and conscious, experiencing the world around you clearly with new eyes and with all your senses but with a mind free of thoughts while experiencing your own consciousness and how it is part of everything.

I'd like to point out that the shift described in the fourth Key, Come Into The Presence Through Your Own Presence, marks a profound cleansing and transformation of consciousness. Therefore, I want to stop for a moment to explain it. The "I" thought ("I think," "I want," "I am") always arises in consciousness; thus, it creates the illusion that consciousness belongs to you. The first three Keys effectively silence thinking in general, and the "I" thought in particular, which sets the stage for this shift in consciousness. When thoughts disappear, concepts like self disappear as well, hence no one remains to own this consciousness. When we stop thinking in terms of "I" and experience our consciousness as part of a greater consciousness that is everywhere and in everything, we realize the Presence itself represents the actual source of all consciousness.

Also, remember experiencing the Presence has nothing to do with what you think. Be clear about this. Do you want to have thoughts about the Presence, or do you want to have an experience of Presence? You decide. Recall Buber's words, "Whether God is transcendent or immanent does not depend on him, it depends on man." It depends on you.

I caution you, though, not to think too much about all this right now, because the moment you do you'll lose awareness of the Presence and wind up back in the World of Man.

Now come back into the exercise by repeating the first four Keys: *Stop Thinking* by repeating these two words to yourself several times. *Intensify Awareness and Perception in the Present* by heightening your awareness and becoming as super-alert as you can, acting as if your life depended upon you doing so. *Experience the World Exactly As It Is* by sharpening your sensory awareness to the extreme and closely examining a specific thing in your personal space. Finally, *Come Into The Presence Through Your Own Presence* by becoming conscious of consciousness itself, and then notice that consciousness exists everywhere – sense space itself as conscious, aware and alive. Focus on that perception. Sense the Presence right now.

Now, in this renewed experience of Presence, silently whisper "God" (or whatever name you prefer) with the longing you feel, the deep desire to experience Divinity. Then, notice what happens. The Hindu poet Kabir says, "It is the intensity of the longing that does all the work." Let there be intensity to your longing, but stay in the sensory mode. Notice the sensory changes you experience as you repeat the divine name.

Meditate and realize this world is filled with the presence of God.
Upanishads (Hindu Scripture)

Continue to focus on the Presence – inside, outside and everywhere, taking all the time you need or want. See if you can sense its nature. For example, you might sense that it is loving, gentle, peaceful, accepting, kind, as soft as light touching your skin and clothes, as gentle as a breeze moving around and through you. Notice, too, how you feel in the Presence, such as safe, ecstatic, joyful, liberated, serene, awe-inspired, or grateful. (Keep in mind that I am just offering a few feelings people experience in the Presence; be sure to trust your own.) And if something about the experience disturbs you, take some time out to understand your reaction. Unpleasant or frightened feelings may be related to negative ideas about the Divine learned in the past. Before continuing, try to identify and release these thoughts and feelings by writing them down or sharing them with a trusted friend or counselor.

Dialogue with the Presence

This next step is both amazing and revelatory. I want you to begin a brief dialogue with the Presence. Try not to question whether this is possible, just follow these directions. Record the conversation on a piece of paper (using your initials and "P" for Presence to indicate who's talking). Start by silently greeting the Presence as you would a beloved friend, and then say what's in your heart. Sense what the Presence says in response. In Judaism, this is called the "Still Small Voice" – God speaking within us. You might hear words that sound like your mind simply talking to you. Do not discount these. Some people say they need to start the process by speaking for the Presence at first – saying something it feels like the Presence would say – until it seems to take over. You might also receive God's response in intuitions, pictures or images in your mind. Record these on the paper. But most importantly, just begin writing a dialogue even if you're not sure what's happening. Continue this interactive process without question or analysis so that the dialogue seems to go on by itself.

And I make it my business only to persevere in His holy presence... an habitual, silent, and secret conversation of the soul with God, which often causes me joys and raptures inwardly, and sometime also outwardly, so great that I am forced to use means to moderate them and prevent their appearance to others.

Brother Lawrence (17th Century Mystic)

Once the dialogue begins, it will feel like a back-and-forth conversation with someone else that just keeps happening. It will feel animated, alive and often surprising. As the conversation unfolds, be sure responses from the Presence come from its consciousness and not from your pre-determined point of view, which will feel like you're just having an increasingly frustrating or boring conversation with yourself. If you are not sure, repeat your statement or question, wait in the silence for a response, and then see what comes from pure consciousness. If your dialogue bogs down in repetitive or abstract ideas, or just seems to go in meaningless circles without being a real back-and-forth interaction, it means you have lost contact with the Presence. In that case, stop the process and either take a break or begin again by repeating the Keys. Then see if the dialogue feels more real. Each person learns this discernment process in his or her own way, so be patient and trust yours.

You might be wondering how a dialogue process is possible when the first Key instructs you to Stop Thinking, so I want to make a distinction here between two uses of thought: impersonal analysis and emotional communication. The first use involves highly intellectual, goal-directed and rather abstract thought processes. It might be called "head-thinking" and works best in understanding material things and complex ideas. The second type uses thought to give expression to personal feelings and truths. It flows from the heart and speaks sincerely about meaningful subjects. With "heart-thinking," we say our truth simply, with feeling and without endless repetition. We need to stop head-thinking to quiet the mind and open to Presence. We use simple and feeling-oriented heart-thoughts next to communicate with the Presence. Here is an example of a dialogue I had recently.

JR: Hello God, are you here?

P: Always.

JR: It feels so good to be close to you again. Thank you for being here with me. You make me feel so happy.

P: It is my greatest pleasure. Happiness is my gift to anyone who knows me. It is my nature.

JR: What is my work today? What should I be doing?

P: Your work is to be with me, to feel me, know me, dissolve into me. Then, all that you do comes from me, and I am you.

JR: Oh, God it is such a relief to let you be me and to let go of the effort to be someone else. And being one with you, nothing matters but this joy.

P: John, I am what you are. Feel my consciousness spreading through you. Feel my Being as your being. Then relax into Me, and I will live you.

JR: But how shall I spend my day? What shall I do?

P: Spend it with me. In Me, all you see and feel becomes holy and beautiful. See with my eyes, and I will show you a new world.

JR: The day is so full. Life is so joyous. It is enough just to breathe and feel the joy of being. I can see that anything I do in this consciousness becomes holy, becomes You, becomes Your work. And this consciousness makes me just love everything, and it is such a tender love. Thank you so much for this.

P: Feel into Me. All that I am is yours. All that I create is yours. As you can see, Heaven spreads everywhere through me

JR: I am overflowing with joy and gratitude. I don't know what to do.

P: Just be with it. It will change you. And as it does, you will know just what to do next. Let it be like a flower blooming. Find the beauty opening all around you. Then you will know who you are and why you're here.

JR: Thank you, God. I love this day. I'm going out for a walk. I will see you everywhere I go.

P: Feel my Presence as you go. That is enough.

Be aware that the most common obstacles to a successful dialogue are skepticism ("I don't believe this can happen.") and the refusal to accept what is intuitively "heard" ("That can't be right."). Most importantly, don't analyze this process while you do it. Later, when you are done, you can decide whether you believe what happened. Finally, be sure to stay in the Presence, repeating the first four Keys whenever you drift back into "head-thinking."

Bidden or not bidden, God is present.
Carl Jung (Psychiatrist, Author)

Return to Everyday Consciousness
When you've finished your dialogue with Divinity, gradually bring your attention and awareness back to ordinary consciousness. Like putting on a familiar suit of clothes, fit back into your everyday thoughts and personality. Feel yourself and your body normally, but notice the difference between the state you experienced while in the Presence and your usual state. This awareness will help you learn more readily to shift in and out of mystical consciousness. Exit sacred space the same way you entered. Blow out your candle, say a prayer or repeat whatever ritual you used at the beginning of this exercise. When you're ready, resume your day's activities in peace and comfort.

Review
Let's find out what happened in this exercise. Answering a few questions about it provides the easiest way to examine and under-

74

stand your experience. What was it like for you?

- Did thinking or skeptical thoughts sabotage your experience?
- Were you able to sense and stay in pure consciousness?
- Was any part of it difficult to accept?
- Could you sense the pure consciousness of Presence?
- What detail of your experience surprised, delighted or enlightened you?
- How did the dialogue go?
- What kinds of discoveries did you make about the nature of Presence?
- Did you learn anything new?
- Could you feel the joy of being in the Presence? What was it like?
- Did this exercise change your experience of the Divine in any way?
- Was this experience so new or different from your customary approach to spirituality that you need some time to reflect on it?

Whatever took place, be sure to reinforce your effort with words of love and appreciation. Point out to yourself the positive or encouraging parts of your experience and express gratitude to yourself and the Presence. Then, when you're ready, repeat the exercise again and again until the experience of Presence comes naturally into your consciousness. If you have difficulty, refer to Appendix B for additional advice and keep trying. The Presence never leaves, and every time you practice, you come closer to experiencing it.

Kabir says: Student, tell me, what is God? He is the breath inside the breath.
Kabir (Hindu Mystic Poet)

Everyday Experiences of Presence

What would happen if you began to practice this exercise of Experiencing the Presence in your everyday life? Jim, one of my spiritual counseling clients, took a real interest in this exercise and did just that. He used it while walking and traveling – even while working, and wrote down some of his remarkable experiences.

Experiencing the Presence during neighborhood walks, Jim described waking up his wonder of everyday life. "The whole experience," he stated, "does, indeed, put me in a different 'place,' since typically in the past I would walk thinking about my work and problem-solving and almost miss any conscious acknowledgement of what was in front of me." Awestruck by the sun's warmth, the diverse smells of freshly cut grass, plants, compost, and the hundreds of shades of green, brown and yellow in the foliage around him, Jim exclaimed, "How delightful! I've seen the spring 64 other times, but am still excited about it." He concluded, "The whole experience leaves me feeling like I've been through some intense meditation," and added that being in the Presence provided him with a "feeling of calm serenity and that things are OK." That was just the beginning.

A consultant, Jim also used this exercise while traveling on business and recalled numerous extraordinary shifts in consciousness over a two-day period. For example, instead of obsessing over his agenda and feeling tense and unprepared before meetings, he said, "I now arrive consciously aware of how serene and calm I feel. I enter the meeting and find myself greeting old colleagues, meeting new individuals, all without any apprehension. I'm joking and laughing." Just as importantly, he related, "The meeting goes quite well extending to five hours, and no one leaves. I'm seldom on my feet for five hours, but I feel great emotionally. Things have gone well. No regrets. No self-criticism. I'm truly taken aback by this...Something is definitely different about this whole experience."

Coming into the Presence while running focus groups, Jim

noted, "This exercise tended to bring me to work refreshed with senses aware and feeling peaceful in a way that I think put others at ease. In this environment, all groups were, shall I say, incredibly forthcoming and civil, and participants felt very good and satisfied about their chance to be 'really heard' on the topics for the first time." He concluded, "I can't be certain, but it seems to me that my approach with these groups – using the Keys – set a non-threatening, non-judgmental environment and produced much richer, honest and useful conversation than would have been the case otherwise. What might be called a spiritually based approach proves to be quite effective in the work place."

Then, on the way home from one business trip, Jim stopped to visit a friend who had recently lost his partner. He recalls, "I sensed a connection with him and a deep appreciation in his eyes – again an exhilarating, yet calming, quiet, and effortless feeling. An experience that I would normally have dreaded – consoling someone in his grief – wasn't that at all. I left promising to keep in touch, as he did, and knew that we would, knew that we had connected with a kind of grace that there is in such things and felt the causeless unconditional joy of it. I had jumped for a brief time from the 'World of Man,' as you call it, over to the 'Heaven on Earth' quadrant of the 'compass' and found it a grand feeling."

On his way home, not far from his friend's apartment, Jim came upon a homeless man, dirty and bedraggled, crouched inside a low box with a sign in front of him asking for charity. Jim recalled, "As usual, I felt compelled to reach in my pocked and give him a couple of one's – only to discover that all I had was $20's. Normally, I would have held back; this time I felt I had to give him a $20. As I asked him how he was, holding the bill through the open 'window,' he arose from the box to his full height – probably about 6' 4" – and smiled a glowing, radiant smile, through the long beard and grime, a much younger man than he appeared. He said, 'I'm much better now, thanks so much. You drive safely and enjoy this beautiful day.' I responded, wishing him the same, thinking that the $20 is too little, and that if there were a 'Presence,' this must be something like it – in him, between us, maybe even in me. It brought tears to my eyes."

On a whim, Jim also stopped to sit and then walk by the ocean and again practiced Experiencing the Presence before going home. He described his experience this way: "The Ocean shimmered with brilliance I hadn't before noticed, hard to gaze at even with dark glasses. After some time – I'm not sure how long – I rose and returned to my car to continue the trip home. Surprise! My body felt rejuvenated, rested, strong, all quite different than before my stop. I felt emotionally strong, a feeling I hadn't had for some time. Just the walk and rest? I don't' think so. I felt like there was something more there...again a movement between quadrants of the compass. Feels great!"

Finally, on another business trip, Jim practiced the exercise in a redwood grove in Northern California. After describing the incredible living beauty of the trees in exquisite detail, he recalled, "The anxiety, agitation and energy I brought into the redwood grove departed, and I felt at ease, pain-free and at peace...even carefree...This placid place was more alive than virtually anywhere I've been – alive, perhaps, with the Presence. I felt at peace, but rejuvenated and strong, as if all this movement, growth and life were within me – was the Presence. How would it be otherwise? And it seemed as if I was at one with my surroundings, and all was as it was, as it should be. With this thought, I suddenly realized I've had none of the 'usual thoughts' since entering and sitting in the grove, and I'd completely lost track of time as we measure it."

Using the Keys to alter his perception, Jim actually began to live in the mystical consciousness of Presence, and doing so began to change everything. This consciousness not only altered his perceptions, it affected those people around him. Experiencing the Presence created a sense of safety, caring and genuine interest that radiated from him and touched and transformed friends, clients and strangers alike. Trusting this new consciousness, Jim also felt more joyous, peaceful, content, and energetic than he had in years. Of course, Jim didn't stay in the experience of Presence every second. He would slip back into ordinary consciousness and have to remind himself to practice the Keys to come back into it. However, fascinated by the world he discovered with these new-found perceptual abilities, Jim had no difficulty motivating himself to keep practicing. And he knew that these everyday experiences of Presence would eventually lead to life in Heaven on Earth.

You, too, can directly sense the Presence anytime you practice the four Keys: Stop Thinking, Intensify Awareness and Perception in the Present, Experience the World Exactly As It Is, and Come into the Presence Through Your Own Presence. In combination with the related dialogue skills, you can learn to experience and converse with the Divine anytime, anywhere. The resulting joy and clarity that will arise in your life will amaze you, for this "Practice of Presence" provides a way of achieving progressive awakening, revelation and ecstasy, and eventually transforms your world.

CHAPTER 7

Transformation

The Cosmos is His form. The forms of the Cosmos are the manifest Reality, He being the manifest. He is also their inner essence, being also the unmanifest...Thou dost not see, in this world or the next, anything beside God...He is Being itself.
Ibn al-'Arabi (13th Century Islamic Scholar, Mystic Philosopher)

Ultimate reality is not a passing moment of bliss, not a fleeting vision or transfiguration, not some ineffable, extraordinary experience or phenomenon but instead is as close as our eyes...I am convinced that we see this reality all our lives but do not recognize it because it is so usual, common, and ordinary that we go off in search of more tantalizing experiences.
Bernadette Roberts (Author)

To grasp God in all things – this is the sign of your new birth.
Meister Eckhart (13th Century Christian Theologian, Mystic)

Introduction
Having understood Heaven's Compass and learned to sense the Presence, you are now ready to embark on a series of experiential exercises intended to transform personal beliefs and problems into experiences of Heaven on Earth. These exercises "solve" problems in an entirely new manner. By bringing the beliefs and feelings that cause problems in our lives through the quadrants of Heaven's Compass, issues dramatically change in ways too extra-ordinary to predict.

It requires no great mental effort but a frequent, quiet pondering on the simple fact of his presence and the habit of directing our inner conversation to him as to a friend who is with us in the dark. The effect will be the gradual substitution of God for our own ego as the goal and center of our thoughts and aspirations.

Anselm Moynihan (Author)

Every time you use Heaven's Compass, be sure to follow the same basic guidelines: Pick a time and place free of interruptions. Have no expectations. Take your time. Experience each step as fully as you can. Resist analyzing or controlling what's happening along the way. And trust what happens. Besides a little bit of time, all you need are a blank sheet of paper and pencil or pen.

This problem-solving process begins by selecting an issue on which to work. The first two steps allow you to experience and express all the relevant facets of the problem. In step one, you write your thoughts and beliefs about the problem in the quadrant labeled "World of Man," for this realm created the problem in the first place. In step two, you record the feelings and emotions created by your thoughts and beliefs in the quadrant labeled "Darkness," which is where we hide our distress. In step three, you come into the Presence and experience its love and peace. Your dialogue with the Presence gradually reveals a new perception of the issue, which you record in the quadrant labeled Divinity. Moving then into the quadrant labeled Heaven on Earth, you practice seeing the divine world and become aware of remarkable new possibilities related to your issue. The steps and contents of this transformational process are summarized below in Figure #3.

World of Man	*Heaven on Earth*
1) Write down the thoughts creating the perceived problem.	4) Practice seeing the world in the Presence as Heaven on Earth. Explore new ways of living in the Presence.
2) Write down the feelings and emotions resulting from problem thoughts.	3) Experience the peace of Presence. Dialogue with Presence then reveals a new spiritual perspective on the problem.
Darkness	*Divinity*

Heaven's Compass as a Practice of Transformation
(Figure # 3)

Exercise: Transforming Your Perception of Reality

Using Heaven's Compass always begins with the selection of a problem on which to work. For this first experience, let's start by applying the fourfold lens of Heaven's Compass to your understanding of reality itself with the goal of identifying and dissolving thoughts and beliefs that conceal Heaven on Earth. Specifically, we want to differentiate between what you think reality is, how these thoughts make you feel, what you learn in the Presence, and, finally, what you actually begin to see in the mystical consciousness of Heaven on Earth.

Step 1. Draw Heaven's Compass: Begin by drawing the intersecting lines of Heaven's Compass on a blank sheet of paper and label each quadrant as I've done in Figure #3. Notice the centering effect of this act, and spend a moment staring at the matrix to focus your awareness. Reflect on the four realms of consciousness represented by these quadrants. Then, at the top of the page write as the title of this exercise the question, "What is reality?" and go on to Step 2. If any of these instructions seem confusing to you, refer to Figure #4 at the end of this section for an illustrative example of the process.

Two years ago a profound dissatisfaction led me to begin trying to line up my actions with the will of God about every fifteen minutes or every half hour... all my waking moments in conscious listening to the inner voice, asking without ceasing, 'What, Father, do you desire said? What, Father, do you desire done this minute?
Thomas Kelly (Quaker Author)

Step 2. Summarize Your Views of Conventional Reality: Begin in the quadrant labeled "World of Man by answering the title question, "What is reality?" Write down all your thoughts on and beliefs about this problem, especially the conventional answers you have been taught including the physical, social, economic, political, religious, and practical definitions. Write short, concise statements and include only what fits in the allotted space. You can use abbreviations or short hand to be succinct.

Step 3. Describe Your Feelings about These Conventional Reality Beliefs: Spend a moment now getting in touch with the feelings triggered by each reality belief. Don't rush this part; feelings come into consciousness at their own pace. You may be surprised by the nature or depth of your feelings. Don't move on until you truly have felt something about your reality beliefs, and then express these feelings as clearly as you can in the quadrant labeled "Darkness."

Step 4. Dialogue with the Presence about Conventional Reality: Now move into the quadrant labeled "Divinity." Begin by becoming quiet and still for a few moments. You may wish to light a candle or say a prayer as a way of facilitating your awareness of the Divine. Next, pull your awareness away from the interpersonal world of people and events into your own personal space – into your body and the 6 to 12 inches around your body. As you do this, try to get centered in your physical being, grounded in its energy and sensations, and to notice the natural rhythm of your breath.

Now move slowly through the four Keys used to come into the Presence, which you learned in the last chapter. Be sure to experience each Key fully before moving onto the next. Here are the keys:

Stop Thinking: Stop thinking and writing, and sit quietly in silence and stillness. Every time your thoughts resume, simply remind yourself, "Stop Thinking!" Practice this first Key for a few moments until it describes your present state of awareness.

In order to practice correctly, you must first have the right thought. The true definition of 'right thought' is 'no thought.' You should not hold onto thoughts of wisdom or vexation because all thoughts, even thoughts of enlightenment, are illusory. 'No thought' is not a blank mind. Someone at the level of 'no thought' is clearly, fully completely aware, and free of illusions.
Master Sheng-yen (Buddhist Author)

Intensify Awareness And Perception in the Present: In the resulting stillness, heighten and sharpen your senses. Become as alert and awake as you possibly can, as if your life depended on it. Practice the first two Keys for a few moments until they describe your present state of awareness.

Experience the World Exactly As It Is: Focus this intensified awareness on the world around you *exactly as it is*, without thought, labels or interpretations. Carefully examine the texture, color and pattern of your skin, clothes or anything nearby. This step involves pure perception without cognition. Practice the first three Keys for a few moments until they describe your present state of awareness.

Come Into the Presence Through Your Own Presence: While still focusing on a specific perception (e.g., your hand or clothing), tune into your own presence at the same time, becoming conscious of consciousness itself. See if you notice a living consciousness all around you filling the stillness and silence of space. Sense this consciousness as you would a living being, because it is. Practice the first four Keys for a few moments until they describe your present state of awareness.

By training yourself to hear the voice of God in everything, the voice reveals itself to your mind as well. Then right in the mind, you discover revelation.
Kabbalah (Jewish Mystical Tradition)

To focus and intensify your experience of Presence, call its name (whatever name feels comfortable to you) silently inside, and notice what changes in your consciousness, feelings, sensory awareness, or surroundings. Try to sense some of the experiential qualities associated with the Presence, including its love, warmth, patience and kindness. Be aware of the feelings that tell you the Presence is near, including spontaneous joy, relief, gratitude, and peace. Stay in the Presence, and let the experience deepen.

Begin Your Dialogue: In the quadrant labeled "Divinity," write a dialogue with the Presence about your reality beliefs and resulting feelings. (Indicate who is speaking by using your initials and "P" for Presence.) Be sure you really sense the Presence before starting. Begin by greeting the Presence as you would a beloved friend and describing how it feels to be together again. Then silently write about what's in your heart. Describe how you feel, ask questions, and trust what comes from the Presence. Let the dialogue become spontaneous – even if you have to start it by speaking for the Presence – until it becomes truly interactive. A real dialogue will be animated, alive and often surprising. Be sure God's words are coming from the experience of Presence and not from your predetermined point of view, which will feel like you're just having an increasingly boring or frustrating conversation with yourself. If your dialogue bogs down in repetitive or abstract ideas, or just seems to go in meaningless circles without being a real back-and-forth interaction, you have lost contact with the Presence. Stop the process and either take a break or repeat the Keys, and see if it feels more real again. Be sure to record the dialogue's flow and what the Presence communicates to you. Stop when the dialogue feels satisfying or complete.

Step 5. See Reality as Heaven on Earth: Now begin to experience Heaven on Earth by completing the following two instructions:

Examine the World in the Presence: Still acutely aware of the Presence, vividly experience the physical environment around you exactly as it is. Do this slowly, deliberately, intently. In other words, see – really see – the colors, textures, patterns, and quality of light in the world, and notice the radiant beauty of things, plants, people, and architecture. Hear – really hear – the sounds of nature, people, things, even silence. Touch – really touch – your own body, clothes, the chair, floor, or walls, and feel the tactile sensations of pressure, texture and temperature as well as of the movement of air in the room. Smell – really smell – the fragrances around you, and see how many you notice. Move around slowly to sense – really sense – your body, its grace, weight, and physical sensations – and experience this physical ground of divine Being. And all through this process, repeat the Stop Thinking Key whenever you drift into worry, criticism, analysis, or comparisons. Stay with naked perception until you discover a pristine world cleansed of distorting ideas and beliefs.

"If this were Heaven on Earth, then...": To further stimulate the perception of Heaven on Earth, simply repeat aloud or in your mind the phrase "If this were Heaven on Earth, then..." and pay close attention to what you see and realize, and answer the following questions:

- What do I see?
- What is reality now?
- How does this reality make me feel?
- If this were truly Heaven, what would it be like?

You also can continue your dialogue with the Presence here to further sharpen your understanding and perception of the divine world. Record your observations and dialogue in the quadrant labeled "Heaven on Earth."

Step 6. Review: Now that you have completed all four quadrants, sit back and review the matrix as a whole. Answer these questions:

- How do your responses differ in each quadrant?
- What do you learn from these differences?
- How has your experience of reality changed?
- How does this exercise make you feel?

Summarize your discoveries on the back of the paper on which you drew your matrix. Then, exit sacred space the same way you entered (blow out the candle or say a prayer). When you're ready, resume your day's activities in peace and comfort.

As amazing as it seems, realize that in your dialogue with Divinity and exploration of Heaven on Earth you actually experienced divine revelation. So, take your discoveries seriously. You are on the threshold of enlightenment.

Example; To help you understand how to use Heaven's Compass, I offer the following personal example. Please don't judge it as better, worse or more "correct" than yours, for everyone's experience carries personal validity, uniqueness and worth.

What Is Reality?

World of Man	*Heaven on Earth* (Creation)
In school I was told that reality was the physical world, solid things you could touch and see. Science classes also told me it was also what physicists and biologists described with their advanced instruments like x-ray machines and microscopes. If you couldn't see it in these ways, it wasn't real. My parents also said that people who needed to believe in things like religion were ignorant, that science could explain everything without needing superstitious ideas like God. Later reality also came to include all that was wrong with the world – political conflict, prejudice, war, poverty, and suffering. I concluded that the only legitimate point of view was the scientific and that my "mystical" perceptions were naïve and foolish.	JR: "If this were Heaven on Earth, then…" Everything is so perfect and amazing and joyous. This is enough! Why did I ever buy into those awful ideas? They felt so painful. What do I do now in this incredible place? P: Just be. Welcome to my Garden. Be one of my divine forms and blossom into your own perfection. Feel yourself, feel the simple bliss of being, and know that you are perfect. I am your life, can you feel me? JR: Oh God, I feel you as my very being and all through me. I feel so happy here with you in this colorful world of light. Thank you for bringing me here. I am so grateful.
These beliefs made me feel wrong and stupid. I felt like I had to give up my mystical side and "grow up." I also felt really sad because these ideas made the world seem like such an awful, hopeless, and depressing place. Why would I want to live in this kind of world? And most of all, this point of view really hurt because it seemed to take away my closeness to God. If there were no God, than my religious needs and longings were childish and wrong. I felt silly and immature for wanting a spiritual life. I hated this way of looking at the world!	JR: Hello God, are you here? P: Always JR: I hate this materialistic point of view. It makes me feel stupid and sad. Is it real? Am I wrong? How do I understand the World of Man's materialism? P: They are just beliefs, John, just ideas, but ideas that are so powerful and convincing. But they are not real, they are just ideas. Let them go and see the world without ideas. Wake up and see this world as Me with all the beauty I put into it. No ideas could ever be as beautiful as every single thing around you. JR: Oh God, it feels so good to release these awful ideas and come home to you. This, now, is real, and it is so incredible. And the joy I feel in your Presence gives me back everything I lost in the World of Man. Thank you for opening my eyes again.
Darkness	Divinity

An Example of Heaven's Compass
(Figure #4)

Let your thoughts flow past you calmly; keep me near, at
every moment; trust me with your life, because I am you,
more than you yourself are.
Bhagavad Gita (Hindu Scripture)

Review: Once again I see how the powerful and convincing ideas constituting the World of Man have controlled and hurt me, causing me to feel guilty and foolish about my natural childhood mysticism. I don't believe that science is wrong. Rather, it represents just one of many ways we experience and understand the world. Incredibly useful in its place, it need not discount spiritual ways of knowing reality. And, as always, I am amazed how good it feels to come back into the Presence and see the world anew.

I use Heaven's Compass nearly everyday to dissolve problems and guide me back into the Presence and to Heaven on Earth. Sometimes my writing fills a whole page, sometimes just a few sentences, and sometimes, when the issue is complex or particularly upsetting; my dialogue can go on for several pages.

Our need is for one thing alone – conscious communion with
God. That is the highest form of prayer, and that form of
prayer can only take place after we have learned, first of all,
that God is, and secondly, that all that exists in this universe
is God 'is-ing'"
Joel Goldsmith (Author)

Beyond the general guidelines given above, this exercise has no "correct" form or outcome. No one grades your work, so feel free to experiment, to take risks, and to learn and grow from your experience. For example, if your dialogue seems unusually long and important, use as many pages as you need. If the process has raised questions for you, Appendix B presents common issues, answers, and other people's experiences to further facilitate your understanding and learning.

Optional Second Round: If the first cycle around Heaven's Compass proved difficult or frustrating, proceed with a second round by following these directions:

Describe Your Thoughts and Feelings: On a clean sheet of paper, draw the lines of Heaven's Compass, and get centered again. Reflect on what bothered you most in the first exercise, summarize it in a title for this new round, write your thoughts in the quadrant labeled "World of Man," and then describe your underlying feelings in the quadrant labeled "Darkness." Be as honest as you can and explore as many thoughts and feelings as you need to.

Dialogue with Presence: Once again use the Keys – Stop Thinking, Intensify Awareness and Perception in the Present, See the World Exactly As It Is, and Come Into the Presence Through Your Own Presence. Greet the Presence as a beloved friend, describe how it feels to be together again, and then begin another dialogue. Describe your concerns and reactions, ask questions and see what emerges from this new dialogue. Notice how your feelings about the exercise evolve in the Presence. Be sure to record the dialogue's flow and what the Presence communicates to you and to stop the dialogue when it feels dry, intellectual or complete.

Return to Heaven on Earth: When you feel ready, look up from your writing and carefully examine the world around you. Staying conscious of the Presence, focus your intense and thoughtless sensory perception on things around you. Notice again how incredibly beautiful, fresh and perfect everything appears. Then, silently repeat the phrase "If this were Heaven on Earth, then…" and see what comes to mind. Continue your dialogue with the Presence if you wish to further discuss Heaven on Earth. Write down your observations or dialogue in the quadrant labeled Heaven on Earth.

Review Again: Ask yourself:
- What did you learn in this second round?
- Did your earlier difficulty dissolve or change?
- Did you learn anything new?
- Are there other worries, fears, skepticism, or negative judgments still blocking your vision?

Remember to pay attention to what *does* happen (not was doesn't), write your responses to the questions and your comments on the back of the paper and save your exercise sheets as a record of your progress. If a large problem or obstacle seems to be blocking your progress, keep working it. With each cycle, another part of the problem will change or dissolve until the problem itself disappears.

Using Heavens Compass to Solve Common Problems

Though you may have begun to glimpse Heaven on Earth in the above exercise, to stay there you'll need to work on a variety of everyday problems. The problems we construct in the World of Man completely block our awareness of Heaven. Every problem consists of a complex fusion of thoughts, beliefs, expectations, attachments, and emotions. The instant you begin struggling with a "problem," you return to the World of Man and get hooked by the unfinished emotions hidden in the Darkness. The more you struggle, the more stuck you become. The discovery of Heaven on Earth arises in a sacred consciousness freed of thought and its consequences, but to get there you need to identify and dissolve each problem as it arises by traveling through the realms of Heaven's Compass.

To use Heaven's Compass as a problem-solving tool, follow the same sequence of steps described above. In brief, select a specific problem – for example, a recent upset, worry, conflict, or painful memory, and then draw Heaven's Compass and place the problem's title at the top of the page. Write your thoughts and beliefs about the problem in the quadrant labeled "World of Man" and your related feelings in the quadrant labeled "Darkness." Next, come into the Presence through the Keys and record your dialogue with the Presence in the quadrant labeled "Divinity." When you're done, move into the quadrant labeled "Heaven on Earth," describe the world you witness in the Presence and complete the sentence "If there were Heaven on Earth, then..." When your work feels complete, review your compass to see what you've learned. Write some of these insights on the back of your sheet of paper. If you still feel troubled or incomplete, consider a second round on the Compass. Finally, remember to exit sacred space the same way you entered. Resume your day's activities in peace and comfort.

In reviewing a problem you've worked on, always consider these kinds of questions:

- How has the problem changed as you moved through the quadrants?
- What did you learn from the Presence about the nature of your problem?
- How does Heaven on Earth return when consciousness clears?
- What do you see and feel as this happens?

Applying Heaven's Compass to everyday problems produces fascinating and rewarding discoveries. Indeed, you may eventually realize that problems don't really need to be "solved" but instead dissolve like smoke into air in the experience of Divinity and Heaven on Earth. Plus, each time you dissolve a problem and glimpse Heaven on Earth in its place, you further "cleanse the doors of perception" and enter an entirely new kind of life.

CHAPTER 8

The Last Veil

The separation of heaven and earth is an image of the birth of consciousness in which humanity is set apart from nature. The self who perceives and values is separated from that which is perceived and evaluated...This new development of consciousness finds expression in the god who orders from beyond rather than the goddess who moves from within.
Anne Baring and Jules Cashford (Jungian Analysts, Authors)

The obstacle is in our 'self,' that is to say, in the tenacious need to maintain our separate, external, egotistic will. It is when we refer all things to this outward and false 'self' that we alienate ourselves form reality and from God.
Thomas Merton (Christian Theologian, Mystic)

Intellectually the self is no more than a psychological concept, a construct that serves to express an unknowable essence which we cannot grasp as such, since by definition it transcends our powers of comprehension. It might equally be called the 'God within us.'"
Carl Jung (Psychiatrist)

Introduction

One more fundamental obstacle must be dismantled on the road to Heaven on Earth. For centuries mystics have called it the "ego" or "self," but this obstacle basically boils down to the "idea of you." As we saw earlier in this book, the idea of you, which I termed the self-concept, forms in the World of Man and becomes its most complicated and compelling illusion. Every major religion seeks to dispel this illusion, because it generates so much selfishness and conflict. If you've been having trouble entering Heaven, it might be because your self-concept needs to be dismantled.

All day long, the self-concept controls and directs us, first with "I" thoughts like "I want...", "I need...", "I should...", and then as increasingly complicated concerns, questions and fantasies, like "Should I do such and such?" "How can I fix this problem?" "What does so and so think of me?" "What if this bad thing happens?" and "Why do people treat me this way?" Each thought and question stimulates the fantasy of a self with a complex life story and endless worries, all of which culminates in the greatest addiction of all: the idea of "you." As this idea stabilizes over the years, it turns into your identity.

We forget that as soon as our thoughts are at peace and all attempts at forming ideas subside, then the Buddha is revealed.
Huang Po (Chinese Philosopher)

While identity can provide the comforting illusion of security and familiarity, change and loss reveal its limitations and trigger our crises. When identity is solidly in place, for example, its recurring thoughts operate as a strait jacket: You only can think what you habitually think, feel what you habitually feel and react as you habitually react. We all know people who never have taken a risk in their lives because of what they feared could go wrong. In this way, identity not only filters ongoing life experiences, it determines your fate. And when an event, like the loss of a job or reorganization at work, disrupts a major part of your identity – such as your income or professional position, overwhelming distress may be triggered simply because of what you think it means to you.

No Self
The idea of self holds so much influence that even questioning its

existence seems absurd. We find it too difficult to even ask, "How can I be an illusion?" Yet, the "I" we're talking about equates to our concept of self – who you *think* you are – not to the *true* self we discover in the Presence.

What would happen, however, if the "I" thoughts were silenced? What if we understood that our identity was an empty fiction? Such questions can be powerfully disarming, for if our identity represents fiction – a made-up story, we have to admit that "I" doesn't really exist except as a figment of our imagination. Like a movie playing in the theater of the mind, we project this "I" story onto every event and interaction. What if the movie ceased? What if the mind were silent?

From the perspective of the infinite, it is obvious that the individual self absolutely does not exist. The idea that we have a self that controls, arbitrates, or is the doer behind our actions is absurd. The individual self is nothing but an idea of who we are. Ideas are ideas – and nothing more. An idea can never be the doer or creator of anything; it can only be what it is – an idea.
Susan Segal (Author)

If we had no "I" thoughts – if the "I" story didn't play inside for any of us, we would have no personal problems to solve, no one to improve, no one to fail, and no one to die. In other words, in the absence of a self-idea the burden of being *somebody* – with all the obligations and expectations that go with identity – simply evaporates. Consciousness doesn't end, but the fiction of being a personal self, separate from others, mortal and problem-ridden, does. For some, this possibility connotes an impossible conundrum for the "I" to solve. But for others, it provides the ultimate freedom, relief and joy.

Because it seems inconceivable, most people find themselves resisting the idea of no self. Organized to perpetuate its own existence, the ego – or "I" thought – creates barriers in the form of doubt, disbelief, worry, fear, and imagined catastrophes. If you believe them, these barriers again become your reality and destiny; in the Presence – without the self-concept – they disappear. Consider complex activities like walking, dancing, driving, or painting. Such activities actually improve when self-consciousness disappears. Nearly everything you now do can be done without a "you" doing it. In psychological language, ego functions continue without the ego. In simple terms, you don't need your ego, your identity, your self-concept, or the belief in "I" – whatever you choose to call it, to do what you do everyday. In fact, you will do everything more easily and more effectively without the ego.

It comes as no surprise that those people who work without ego are extraordinarily successful at what they do. Anybody who is one with what he or she does is building the new earth.
Eckhart Tolle (Modern Mystic)

Who Lives in Heaven on Earth?

If no personal identity exists in the Presence, one might wonder, "Who lives in Heaven on Earth?" The answer is the "divine self," that unique combination of love, talent, consciousness, and knowing that reflects Divinity being you. Psychologists and psychiatrists call this "the true self," while those coming from a spiritual viewpoint call it "the soul" or the "higher self." Entirely separate from the self-concept, the divine self fills us in times of joy, love and creativity when it overflows the restrictive rules and beliefs of identity. Unconditionally generous and compassionate, the divine self finds injustice intolerable, for its experience of divine unity – we are all part of the One – understands that whatever happens to another is happening to me as well, and hence cannot be ignored. In its highest manifestation, known as the Cosmic Christ, Buddha Mind, or a thousand other names, the divine self reflects the infinite divine consciousness channeled into finite experience through you. In other words, "you" are part of God living in and through "your" consciousness and being. Identity, it turns out, has simply been a distorting lens that, once wiped clean, allows the light of Divinity to shine through you and everything else. In sum, who you think you are is what separates you from God, and where you think you are is what separates you from Heaven on Earth.

This consciousness is the universal consciousness – that is, the feeling of Presence. When one sees the situation as it really is, that no individual is involved, that what is present is Presence as a whole and merely the expression of the Absolute, then the moment this is perceived there is liberation.
Nisargadda Maharaj (Hindu Sage)

Finally, keep in mind that dissolving the "I" thought and its manufactured identity occur as a gradual process, and we often remain in various intermediate states for a very long time. For example, sometimes you may wonder whether your consciousness has filled with the Divine or actually become the Divine. At other times, "you" disappear altogether and Divinity looks through "your" eyes. Still other times, the Divine seems to use "you" to express its creativity, love or social action. Sometimes, too, you discover that "your" boundaries have expanded to include all of Creation as "you." Learning to be in the Presence and live in Heaven on Earth, therefore, represents a fluid and evolving process that takes on many forms as it moves toward its fulfillment (self-concept, no self, divine self, self as world). What an amazing adventure! The culmination of this process results in such divine beings as Jesus, Buddha, Lao Tzu, Ramakrishna, and countless other mystics, known and unknown, all of whom realized no self as a stage in the embodiment of Divinity as their true identity. One day you will, too.

The idea of no self, of course, can be threatening to people rigidly identified with their self-concept. For them, being "nobody" can be frightening or depressing. They also may believe that anyone experiencing the divine self must be crazy, grandiose or power hungry – ideas naturally projected by one still trapped in the idea of self. In the emptiness of no self, however, no one exists to be crazy, grandiose or power hungry. Instead Divinity fluidly manifests in individual being and consciousness. In fact, it is from our common divine nature that we realize we are all one, that the Divine lives in every creature and that self-and-other represents an illusion.

All that divides us from the sea of infinite consciousness at this point is a thin envelope of personal identity.
Eknath Easwaran (Indian-American Philosopher and Meditation Teacher)

Exercise: Experiencing No Self with Heaven's Compass

Experiencing no self, or its equivalent — the divine self, is easier than the mystical literature implies. Such mystical realization need not come after decades of intense spiritual practice and lofty visions. Like Heaven on Earth, it always exists and Heaven's Compass can point the way so anyone can find it. I've designed this exercise so you can use Heaven's Compass to do just that – find no self. Try it and see happens to your self-concept.

As before, be sure to follow the same basic guidelines: Pick a time and place free of interruptions. Have no expectations. Take your time. Experience each step as fully as you can. Resist analyzing or controlling what's happening along the way. And trust what happens. All you need are a blank sheet of paper and pencil or pen.

Step 1. Draw Heaven's Compass: Begin by drawing the intersecting lines of Heaven's Compass on a blank sheet of paper and identifying the quadrants. Notice the centering effect of this act and spend a moment staring at it to focus your awareness. Reflect on the four realms of consciousness represented by the quadrants. Pick an appropriate title for this exercise, and write it at the top of the page.

> *Divine I am inside and out, and I make holy whatever I*
> *touch and am touched by.*
> Walt Whitman (Poet)

Step 2. Summarize Your Beliefs About Your Self: In the quadrant labeled "World of Man," briefly summarize all the ideas you have about yourself – your identity, past and present life story, hopes and fears, best and worst qualities, and anything else you think of as "you." Or begin with the phrase "I am," and list all the things you believe about your self. For example, you might write, "I am a man, a father, an accountant, a mortal, a seeker, worried about such and such, thinking this and that," and so on. Use broad concepts in place of endless details to conserve space and time. This description represents who you *think* you are. You might also explore the parts of your self-concept or life story you would be most pleased to give up as well as the parts you are most attached to and would grieve to surrender. Write short, concise statements and include only what fits in the allotted space. You can use abbreviations or short hand to be succinct

Step 3. Describe Feelings Caused by Your Self-Concept: Spend a moment getting in touch with the feelings triggered by your descriptions above. Don't rush this part; feelings come into consciousness at their own pace. You may be surprised by the nature and depth of your feelings. Don't start writing until you have truly felt something about your self-concept. Then, in the quadrant labeled "Darkness," describe the feelings evoked by these ideas about your self. If you feel stuck, you can begin with "I feel" and then list all the feelings you discover. For example, you might write, "I feel sad, tired, bored, lonely, unsure of myself," and so on. Finally, describe how it would feel to be "nobody." While doing so, consider the questions, "Why would that be a problem?" and "How might it also feel like a relief?"

Step 4. Dialogue with the Presence about Your Self-Concept: Now move into the quadrant labeled "Divinity." Begin by becoming quiet and still for a few moments. You may wish to light a candle or say a prayer as a way of facilitating awareness of sacred space. Next, pull your awareness away from the interpersonal world of people and events and into your own personal space – that is, into your body and the 6 to 12 inches around your body. As you do this, try to get centered in your physical being, grounded in its energy and sensations, and notice the natural rhythm of your breathing.

Now move slowly through the four Keys used to come into the Presence that you learned in Chapter 6, which I have described briefly again below. Be sure to experience each Key fully before moving onto the next. Here are the Keys:

Stop Thinking: Stop thinking and writing, and sit quietly in silence and stillness. Every time your thoughts resume, simply remind yourself, "Stop Thinking!" Practice this first Key for a few moments until it becomes your present state of awareness.

Intensify Awareness And Perception in the Present: In the resulting stillness, heighten and sharpen your senses. Become as alert and awake as you possibly can, as if your life depended on it. Practice the first two Keys for a few moments until they describe your present state of awareness.

Experience The World Exactly As It Is: Focus this intensified awareness on the world around you *exactly as it is,* without thought, labels or interpretations. Carefully examine the texture, color, and pattern of your skin, clothes, or anything nearby. This step involves pure perception without cognition. Practice the first three Keys for a few moments until they describe your present state of awareness.

Come Into The Presence through Your Own Presence: While still focusing on a specific perception (e.g., your hand or clothing), tune into your own presence at the same time, becoming conscious of consciousness itself. See if you notice a living consciousness all around you filling the stillness and silence of space. Sense this consciousness as you would a living being, because it is. Practice the first four Keys for a few moments until they describe your present state of awareness.

To focus and intensify your experience of Presence, call its name (whatever name feels comfortable to you) silently inside and notice what changes in your consciousness, feelings, sensory awareness, or surroundings. Try to sense some of the experiential qualities associated with the Presence, including its love, warmth, patience, and kindness. Be aware of the feelings that tell you the Presence is near, including spontaneous joy, relief, gratitude, and peace. Stay in the Presence and let the experience deepen.

You are simply a channel for the divine attributes... You have no independent self and are contained in the Creator.
Kabbalah. (Jewish Mystical Tradition)

Begin Your Dialogue: In the quadrant labeled "Divinity," write a dialogue with the Presence about your self-concept beliefs and resulting feelings. (Again, use your initials and "P" for Presence to indicate who is speaking). Be sure you really feel the Presence before starting. Begin by greeting the Presence as you would a beloved friend and describing how it feels to be together again.

Then silently write about what's in your heart. Describe how you feel, ask questions, and trust what comes from the Presence. Let the dialogue become spontaneous – even if you have to start it by speaking for the Presence – until it becomes truly interactive. A real dialogue will be animated, alive and often surprising. Be sure God's words are coming from the experience of Presence and not from your predetermined point of view, which will feel like you're just having an increasingly boring or frustrating conversation with yourself. If your dialogue bogs down in repetitive or abstract ideas, or just seems to have lost contact with the Presence, stop the process and either take a break or repeat the Keys and see if it feels more real again. Be sure to record the dialogue's flow and what the Presence communicates to you. Stop the dialogue when it feels satisfying or complete.

In my soul, God not only gives birth to me as His son, He gives birth to me as Himself, and Himself as me.
Meister Eckhart (13th Century Theologian, Mystic)

Step 5. See Reality as Heaven on Earth: Once again move into the quadrant labeled "Heaven on Earth" and follow these instructions:

Examine the World in the Presence; Still acutely aware of the Presence, vividly experience the physical environment around you exactly as it is. Do this slowly, deliberately, intently, using whichever sense (seeing, listening, touching, smelling, moving) brings you most clearly into the sensory here-and-now. And all through this process, repeat the Stop Thinking Key whenever you drift into worry, criticism, analysis, or comparisons. Let this pure, crystal-clear consciousness perceive the matchless beauty of Heaven on Earth.

Experience the Divine Self: Now explore the following experiences of the divine self, remaining with any one of them as long as you like.

1. Turn this sharpened awareness onto the body – sense your physical being – and thrill with the discovery that it is part of the divine Being. You are made of God.
2. Feel your divine self and sense its many gifts or energies and how they wish to be expressed through you at this very moment.
3. Realize that Divinity is looking through "your" eyes into Creation, hearing with "your" ears, touching with "your" hands. What does it see, feel or want to do?
4. Consider the possibility that "you" are all that is, one single existence with nothing separated from anything else, all an extension of Divinity. Feel "your" oneness with Creation.

As you tap into the divine self with its many variations, see what happens next. Who are you now? And now? And now?

"If this were Heaven on Earth, then...": To further stimulate the perception of Heaven on Earth, simply repeat the phrase, "If this were Heaven on Earth, then...," and pay close attention to what you see and realize. Write down your observations of the divine world. Ask yourself:

• What do I see?
• How does it feel to be centered in the divine self?
• What do I feel like doing from this consciousness?

Record your observations and dialogue in the quadrant labeled "Heaven on Earth." You may also continue your dialogue with the Presence here.

Step 6. Review: Before completing this exercise, ask yourself the following questions:

- How did your self-experience change in each quadrant?
- How does your self-concept seem different now?
- What else do you understand or notice about the no self/divine self experience?
- What new insights occur to you about the self?

And consider these questions:

- How is pure consciousness different from self-consciousness?
- How does it feel being centered in pure consciousness without being anyone?
- What happens when you open to the divine Presence as your own presence?

Summarize your discoveries on the back of the paper on which you drew your matrix. Finally, exit sacred space the same way you entered. Resume your day's activities in peace and comfort.

Conclusions

The assumption of a self-concept – the belief that you are a separate object, entity or thing that must struggle to overcome its inherent faults, vulnerabilities and mortality – serves as the original and most tragic mistake of the spiritual life. Erasing this self-concept dissolves the whole fiction of identity, time and story. In this way, no self/divine self becomes the final and ultimate healing and the last veil to Heaven on Earth. When you see through the eyes of Divinity, all you see is divine.

Practice experiencing no self/divine self during the day. You can do this by coming into the Presence and silently asking, "Who talks?" "Who thinks?" "Who drives?" "Who is hungry?" or "Who is upset?" Then, sense the reply coming from Divinity. Feel the impulse to move beyond the limitations of the self-concept, and go with it. Notice, too, that life proceeds quite easily without the idea of a separate self as actor, thinker, feeler, or doer. It simply flows.

Finally, as your self-transformation unfolds, try to discover how you know and express Divinity in "your" life. Ask yourself, "What does my divine self want or feel?" And remember, no absolute rules for this realization exist, and no one can dictate your result. Just trust and live what you discover. In the next chapter, you will learn how myth, fairy tale, and real life stories also portray the universal themes and cycles of spiritual life.

CHAPTER 9

Story Time

Myths are stories of our search through the ages for truth, for meaning, for significance...Myths are clues to the spiritual potentialities of the human life.
Joseph Campbell (Mythologist)

The reason for the ageless appeal of fairy tales can be summed up in an old Hasidic proverb: give people a fact or an idea and you enlighten their minds; tell them a story and you touch their souls.
Allan Chinen (Jungian Psychiatrist)

A living myth, like an iceberg, is 10 percent visible and 90 percent beneath the surface of consciousness.
Sam Keen (Author)

Introduction
After the challenge of reading the last eight chapters, you're earned a break. So, I want to tell you three remarkable stories that describe Heaven on Earth from a different perspective. See if you can intuit their symbolic meanings, particularly in light of the journey described by the cycles of Heaven's Compass.

Why Coyotes Bay at the Moon
The first tale, actually a myth, comes from the Pueblo Indians living near Santa Fe, New Mexico. True to the oral tradition, I heard it from a friend many years ago. He told me:

Soon after the Great Spirit made this world, one night he was sitting alone gazing up into the dark and empty sky, which contained no moon, stars or light of any kind. He saw nothing but pitch-black nothingness. After a long while, the Great Spirit looked for Po-Say-Wa, the coyote, whose name means "one who hangs his head."

Po-Say-Wa quickly responded – you don't ignore the Great Spirit. The Great Spirit presented him with a large leather bag tied tightly with sinew, and said, "You must take this bag, and follow the trail that winds through the mountains and deserts. Open the bag only when you get to the end of the journey, not before. Your travels may be long and hard, but you are not to stop until you reach your destination."

The fact that the Great Spirit had picked him for such a great assignment surprised Po-Say-Wa. He was, after all, not highly regarded by the other creatures of the world. Perhaps it was because he sneaked around scavenging for food and taking anything he could find – sometimes even taking it from others. Thrilled by this great honor, Po-Say-Wa began his journey – head up, feeling important and determined.

Days and nights, nights and days, Po-Say-Wa journeyed onward, and the trail was indeed long and hard. He crossed steep rocky cliffs, dry and barren deserts. As time went by, Po-Say-Wa began to lose both his sense of pride and his resolve. One evening, as the sky grew dark and hunger crowded out ambition, Po-Say-Wa began to chew absent-mindedly on the sinew securing the bag. It was delicious! Hungry for more, he kept on chewing. As darkness fell, he realized he had eaten all the sinew.

Suddenly, the leather bag burst open. "Oh what have I done?" he cried. Then, to Po-Say-Wa's astonishment, out from the bag flew clouds of glittering mica. Just as quickly, the mica's glowing flakes floated into the night sky, spreading out to become a canopy of sparkling stars. And then a huge ball of mica rose from the bag, taking its place in the sky as the moon. "Oh, my God," whispered Po-Say-Wa in awe and fear.

As Po-Say-Wa looked up at the sky, he only could think of how he had failed the Great Spirit by opening the bag before reaching the *trail's end. The night grew cold, and Po-Say-Wa shivered in despair. Finally, full of shame and disappointment, he raised his head and let out a sorrowful cry to the on-looking heavens. The Pueblo Indians say this is why coyotes walk with their tails dragging and heads hung low. When they see the moon gazing down on them with its accusing look, they cry out in shame and sorrow.*

Sacred stories move us; they get us thinking about what is important; they communicate through symbol and metaphor deep truths about the mysteries of life. Upon hearing a sacred story, even if we don't understand the message intellectually, we are aware that some profound lesson has been imported.
Charles and Ann Simpkinson (Publishers of Common Boundary)

Interpretation

This story suggests that Divinity entrusts each of us, no matter how lowly or unimportant we seem, with something infinitely precious to deliver on our long and winding journey through life. It tells us that somehow, even in our apparent failure, we give birth to the Divine and fill the world with its beauty.

Symbolically, like Po-Say-Wa, we each carry the precious treasure of the divine self entrusted to us by the Great Spirit and filled with the gifts we are meant to bring into the world. And, like Po-Say-Wa, we, too, become distracted by the self-idea and its grandiose fantasies and spend years in prideful posturing in the World of Man. Eventually, however, we grow weary of carrying this burden of the self-concept and start gnawing to get at what's really inside. To get at this hidden treasure, our grandiose outer mission in the World of Man must fail so we can explore the "bag" of Darkness within ourselves. The miracle, of course, comes next. In opening the medicine bag of our soul, we release our Divinity to the world, thus contributing to the beauty of Heaven on Earth that we all are meant to share.

Sadly, the defeat of the false self in the World of Man often makes us believe that we have failed. Po-Say-Wa represents that part of us that doesn't yet comprehend and celebrate the value of dismantling the inflated self-concept – who we think we are or should be – and that doesn't yet realize that this allows us to express our divine self instead. If he could relinquish the negative beliefs that caused him to feel lowly in the first place, Po-Say-Wa would realize quickly the glorious role he played in the building of Heaven on Earth. If we followed suit, we might do the same.

The Prodigal Son

The fifteenth chapter of the Gospel of Luke offers an allegory of our circular journey through the quadrants of Heaven's Compass to arrive in Heaven itself. A story from the Christian scriptures, it goes like this:

There once was a certain man who had two sons. One day the younger son said to his father, "Father, give me the share of your wealth that falls to me." So, the father divided his livelihood between the two. Not many days afterwards, the younger son gathered his share and journeyed to a distant country, and there wasted his money on a life of irresponsible living.

When he had spent all his wealth, there arose a severe famine in that land, and the son fell into want. So, he enjoined himself to a citizen of that country and was sent into his fields to feed swine. He gladly would have filled his own stomach with the pods that the swine ate, but no one gave him anything.

Finally, he came to himself, and said, "How many of my father's hired servants have bread enough to spare, and I perish with hunger! I will arise and go to my father, and will say to him, 'Father, I have sinned against heaven and before you, and I am no longer worthy to be called your son. Make me like one of your hired servants.'"

And he arose and came to his father, but when he was still a great way off, his father saw him and had compassion. He ran straight away to his son and kissed him. The son said to him, "Father, I have sinned against heaven and in your sight and am no longer worthy to be called your son."

We turn to mythology because myth is the language that most closely approximates the natural workings of the psyche... A mythic outlook also reminds you that you are part of a larger picture than your immediate concerns.
David Feinstein and Stanley Krippner
(Psychologists, Authors)

The father said to his servants, "Bring out the best robe and put it on him, and put a ring on his hand and sandals on his feet. Bring the fatted calf here, and kill it, and let us eat and be merry for my son was dead and is alive again; he was lost and is found." And they began to be merry.

Now the elder son was in the field and on his way home heard music and dancing. He culled one of the servants and asked what was going on. The servant explained, "Your brother has come home, and your father has killed the fatted calf, because he is safe and sound." The older brother became angry and would not go in.

His father came outside and pleaded with him, but the older son argued, "All these many years I have served you. Never have I disobeyed your commandments, and you never gave me so much as a kid that I might make merry with my friends. Yet, as soon as my brother, who has wasted all your money on harlots, comes home, you kill the fatted calf for him."

His father replied, "Son, you are always with me, and all I have is yours. How could we not celebrate this happy day, for your brother was dead and has come back to life, was lost and now is found."

Interpretation
This, too, represents a story about a journey. We recognize it as a religious story because of its source, and we understand its

symbolic nature because Jesus typically spoke in parables. Even though it never directly mentions the Divine, we can assume safely that the figures in the story represent the relationship between humankind (the sons) and God (the father).

The sons in this parable symbolize two very different ways of relating to the Divine and journeying to Heaven on Earth. One son clings to the rules of the father, believing that perfect compliance will be rewarded. He has created his own World of Man built on rules, appearances, comparisons, entitlement, and secret superiority. Representing that part of us that adopts the "good boy/good girl" version of the false self, he insists on being rewarded. The younger son, though also caught in the illusory World of Man, goes in search of adventure amongst life's myriad experiences and sensations. Unlike the older son, he risks the journey of life and eventually learns its universal lessons.

God, the father, gives the younger son half his "livelihood," literally that which he lives by – a symbol of the divine gift of life and soul. The son takes this gift, travels far, and like all of us, winds up squandering too much of it on the material ambitions and acquisitions in the World of Man. "Severe famine" provides a powerful simile for the hunger, desperation and helplessness that grow in a life driven by materialism alone. Feeling less than a lowly swine, he descends into the deep, dank, fecund mud of Earth. While the older son remains stuck in the World of Man the younger son now moves into the realm of Darkness.

For the Australian as well as the Chinese, the Hindu and the European peasant, the myths are true because they are sacred, because they tell him about sacred beings and events. Consequently, in reciting or listening to a myth, one resumes contact with the sacred and with reality, and in so doing one transcends the profane condition, the "historical situation."
Mircea Eliade (Anthropologist, Author)

The story then refers to the moment the prodigal son finally "came to himself," an incisive reference to the rediscovery of the true self. In his reconnection to self and soul, the youth's thoughts naturally return to God – in this case, his father. Realizing that the journey from his father had caused his suffering, the son decides to return home, admit his error and seek forgiveness. Asking to be a servant expresses a profound humility that corrects his earlier inflation. Coming home to his father, thus, represents his desire for re-union with Divinity.

God has been waiting, looking forward to the day his prodigal son will hit bottom, lose interest in the World of Man and return home. Thus, in this allegory, the father feels overjoyed when he sees his son approaching and treats him to all the riches he has to offer. In this symbolic homecoming, God's gift of divine life is fully restored to the son who is, in effect, born anew in the Kingdom of God, for Heaven on Earth appears whenever we are in the sacred Presence.

The elder son, however, cannot understand his father's joy and generosity. Like anyone trapped in the World of Man, he wants life to conform to his rules and expectations. He also feels considerable – albeit unconscious – pain, because his rigidity interferes with a truly loving relationship with the Divine. The older son argues indignantly, and his bitterness only serves to maintain his separation and alienation.

Unlike Coyote or the elder brother, the prodigal son not only completes the first cycle around Heaven's Compass by recovering true self and soul, he also completes the second cycle by returning to spirit. He now lives in the experience of Heaven on Earth created by God's Presence. Stuck in shame, Coyote never returns to the Great Spirit for forgiveness or reunion, and, stuck in his arrogance, the elder son never surrenders his need to be right. The prodigal son willingly gives up identity and control to find Divinity and Creation – right where he left it.

The Man Who Found – and Lost – Heaven on Earth

The third story I'm going to tell you is a true one about a man who actually found and then lost Heaven on Earth. It happened this way:

Alexander Selkirk, a hot-tempered Scot frequently in trouble with the authorities, joined the crew of an armed merchant ship out of Ireland for a life of privateering, or government-sanctioned pirating common at the turn of the eighteenth century. Sailing down the western coast of South America, the ship stopped at Mas-a-Tierra, a deserted island, to replenish its supplies of fresh water, fruit and meat. The voyage had been long, harsh and largely unsuccessful, and the ship was badly in need of repair. Tempers flared on board, and a new captain, known for his tyrannical and arrogant leadership, took charge. One day, Selkirk could no longer hold his temper and impulsively demanded to be left ashore. To his enormous shock and dismay, he got his wish.

In the eight months that followed that ill-fated day in September of 1704, Selkirk lived in terror, regret and melancholy. Unwilling to take his eyes off the horizon, he stayed by the shore surviving on shellfish and turtles. However, when he was driven inland by hoards of aggressive sea lions, he discovered a land of abundant fruit, herds of goats and plentiful firewood. As winter arrived, he built two small huts, befriended dozens of cats (which kept the rats away), and made a life for himself reading the Bible he had brought ashore, exploring the island, and playing with his new "friends." Goatskins replaced tailored clothes; calloused feet replaced shoes. Selkirk became so fit and strong he could actually chase down prey for supper. Though he dreamed of rescue, Selkirk gradually came to love this place and eventually reconciled himself to living out the rest of his life here. In fact, his solitude had become a spiritual path that led him back to Paradise.

In 1709, four years and four months after Selkirk's abandonment, another English privateering vessel appeared, dropped anchor and discovered a wild man dressed in sheepskins unable to speak intelligibly. Recognized by one of the crew, Selkirk was taken on board and gradually resumed the life of a sailor. He remained on the ship for another two years before finally reaching London in 1711. Unlike his first ship, this vessel's years of plundering had been most lucrative, and Selkirk returned to civilization a rich man. His story of being marooned on a desert island also made him a celebrity and served as the basis of the fabulously successful tale of Robinson Crusoe.

A rich and famous man with all he could ever want, Alexander Selkirk should have been happy, but he wasn't. Two years after his homecoming, an interviewer observed, "The man frequently bewailed his return to the world, which could not, he said, with all its enjoyments, restore to him the tranquility of his solitude." Selkirk himself concluded to the interviewer, "I am now worth eight hundred pounds, but shall never be so happy as when I was not worth a farthing."

Interpretation

What really happened to Alexander Selkirk? He found Heaven on Earth on the deserted island of Mas-a-Tierra. After completely losing the World of Man and finally working through the emotional pain of this enormous loss – his journey through Darkness, he settled into a paradise untouched by time, identity, personal worth, or human conflict. Focusing on Divinity through his Bible reading, and experiencing it through the expansion of his consciousness, Selkirk's world became Creation once again and he lived like Adam.

Sadly, the one illusion Selkirk never surrendered was the idea that true happiness could only be found in civilization, but, in the end, he could not find it there. With drink and morbid nostalgia, his melancholy grew. Finally, in 1720, Selkirk signed on with another ship only to die of yellow fever at sea a year later.

Selkirk's greatest mistake came in his failure to realize that

Heaven on Earth lies everywhere. Confusing the consciousness of Creation awakened on a desert island with the island itself, he lost his capacity to see the divine world elsewhere. Dwelling on the past then assured he would never reawaken to the timeless present that had revealed Heaven on Earth to him in the first place. Selkirk remained psychologically marooned in the World of Man until his death.

Conclusions

Since Heaven's Compass and mythology both reveal the archetypal structure of consciousness, these stories readily describe the journey we all take away from the divine world and back again. This circular and cyclical adventure of betrayal, descent, reunion, and renewal creates the seasons and cycles of life, and the way we eventually come home to Heaven on Earth. Most of us remain trapped in the concepts, beliefs and fantasies comprising the World of Man. Some, like the elder son, never leave. Others, like Coyote and Alexander Selkirk, travel part way around the realms of Heaven's Compass only to get trapped again in another illusory dead end in the World of Man. The prodigal son, however, takes us all the way home, illustrating the ultimate journey to Heaven on Earth.

CHAPTER 10

Living in Heaven on Earth

No heaven can come to us unless our hearts find rest in today. Take Heaven. No peace lies in the future which is not hidden in the present little instant. Take Peace. There is radiance and glory in the darkness could we but see, and to see we have only to look. I beseech you to look. Life is so generous a giver, but we, judging its gifts by the covering, cast them away as ugly or heavy or hard. Remove the covering and you will find beneath it a living splendor woven of love, by wisdom, with power...you will find earth but cloaks your heaven. Courage, then, to claim it, that is all. But courage you have, and the knowledge that we are all pilgrims together, wending through unknown country, home.

Fra Giovanni, 1513 A.D.
(16th Century Priest and Scholar)

Introduction

Living in Heaven on Earth represents an art, and, as any artist will tell you, developing the necessary skills to create art takes time, patience and practice. Although the sometimes-lengthy process involves inspiration and mistakes, excitement and setbacks, disappointment and renewed determination, discouragement and ever-increasing proficiency, one day the art of living in the Presence becomes second nature and Heaven on Earth becomes your home.

As with any new home, it's nice to have an inkling of what life there might involve. Therefore, I'd like to describe for you life in Heaven on Earth as well as the challenge of living in two worlds – Heaven on Earth and the World of Man. In addition, in this chapter I will present our final exercise, called "Take Heaven."

"A new heaven" is the emergence of a transformed state of human consciousness, and "a new earth" is its reflection in the physical realm.
Eckhart Tolle (Author, Modern Mystic)

Everyday Life in Heaven on Earth

As we begin to live more and more in the mystical consciousness of Heaven on Earth, our lives change in many ways. In fact, as you've practiced the exercises in this book, you may have found that yours has changed already in small – or even significant – ways. While everyone experiences living in the Presence in a slightly different manner, your everyday life might include the following experiences:

Life is simpler, happier and moves forward at its own slower, natural and almost effortless pace and with its own natural rhythms. Past, present and future – indeed, all aspects of time – dissolve in the same way that all fixed ideas dissolve in the experience of Presence. Your everyday activities – time with family, going to work, doing chores, exercising, and paying bills – continue as always; they may even look the same from the outside, but internally you now experience them as part of the mystery, timelessness and perfection of existence. You realize the world doesn't need to be anything different than what it already is in the mystical here and now. Practical elements from the World of Man, such as clocks, currency and language, remain useful tools but no longer dominate your life.

Living in the Presence with no self-concept to fix, prove or defend, your old problems of identity, worth and purpose fade away. You no longer wait for some special event to improve your life or self-esteem. Instead, the pleasure of living each moment in Heaven on Earth replaces the habit of turning circumstances into personal problems or seeking something else to make you happy or whole. Indeed, most problems seem to resolve or fade away by themselves in the experience of Presence. Gossip and complaining naturally give way to awe and gratitude as the most genuine responses to living in the divine world. The magic of love, trust, wonder, adoration, and joy replace concerns – actually illusions – about ambition, motivation, productivity, social standing, physical appearance, and money.

The Kingdom of God... is not situated in space and time. You do not have to die in order to enter the Kingdom of God; in fact you are already in it now and here. The only thing is that you don't know it.
Thich Nhat Hanh (Buddhist Monk, Teacher, Author)

People, animals and things become increasingly beautiful, and you find yourself endlessly delighted and amazed by the unfathomable mystery of the world. In this heavenly experience, the simplest actions, such as touching, walking, playing, loving, helping, and listening, become sources of immense pleasure, interest, satisfaction, and fascination. For you, the world has transformed into a wonderland of physical and emotional delight.

Learning to experience the Divine ever more fully becomes your abiding goal and pleasure – and you realize everything in Creation reaches out to you for this purpose. Indeed, freed from the illusions of identity, time and story, reality shines forth as Divinity. Exploring the world now involves ever-increasing contact with the Divine and its infinite intelligence, which provides you with a deeply and inherently reinforcing experience.

When living in Heaven on Earth, Divinity not only offers its comforting and healing Presence everywhere, it increasingly fills your own presence. Life then unfolds on the pathless path of Self-realization – of just being what you are, which flows with wonder, love, creativity, and celebration. Pronouns like "I" or "you" are used for conventional reference but no longer signify a self-concept concerned with personal worth or control. Consciousness expands into a present-moment awareness – you are in the "now" – without big goals, plans or agendas. With no self-concept to divide one person from another, you also discover that everyone embodies the same divine Being that has happily refracted into endless variations. Relationships transform with the joy of sharing this oneness rather than the posturing of separate false selves.

No sin, evil, guilt, illness, suffering, or ugliness exist in Heaven on Earth, nor any legalistic rules for behavior. The joy and appreciation of divine life are so immediate that you require no rules, commandments or dogma. You no longer cloak the body in dualistic categories – good-bad, sick-well, young-old, able-disabled, attractive-unattractive – that offered painful misconceptions in the World of Man. With consciousness less and less identified with concepts of body, self and survival, your fear of dying diminishes greatly. Understanding that death represents a further surrendering of illusions as you move into yet another great cycle creates a wondrous and holy ending on this plane. Living in harmony with the flow and dynamics of Creation – of birth and death, seasons and cycles – you learn to trust the inherent order of the universe and honor its rhythms in your life through ritual and celebration.

Compassion, forgiveness, patience, generosity, and love grow naturally from your new consciousness of Presence and include all beings. As you experience the joy of Heaven on Earth, the desire to help others escape the conceptual tyranny of the World of Man arises naturally within you. Though most around you remain convinced of its illusions, the joy of helping provides reinforcement enough for you to persist in your efforts.

Finally, whatever its form and function, the work you find in Heaven on Earth overflows with creativity and love, thus contributing to the beauty and fullness of Creation. Your work originates from the unique gifts of your divine self, making it intrinsically interesting, satisfying and necessary to the building of Heaven on Earth. As you and others in the Presence nourish every gift, you each ensure that the community as a whole also prospers. You no longer experience boredom or unemployment, since neither exists in Heaven on Earth.

This earth and all that is in it, and the whole cosmic order to which it belongs, has to undergo a transformation; it has to be come a "new heaven and a new earth."... This is the ultimate goal of human history and of the created universe.....Our present world is conditioned by our present mode of consciousness; only when that consciousness passes from its present dualistic mode conditioned by time and space will the new creation appear... "

Bede Griffiths (Catholic Monk, Indian Scholar, Author)

The Challenge of Living in Two Worlds

Living in Heaven on Earth requires competence in two worlds simultaneously: the conventional World of Man, in which others function, and Heaven on Earth, which erases all the lines, beliefs, identities, and accepted meanings of the conventional world. The challenge involves learning how to move through the World of Man without falling back into its illusions – in the words of Jesus, being "in the world but not of it." Interestingly, the essence and definition of an enlightened being consists of living in two worlds. The mystic, shaman, bodhisattva, and spiritual elder all reflect variations of this state of consciousness, but achieving enlightenment also presents the following challenges:

Conversation: In Heaven on Earth, conventional ideas and beliefs are experienced as illusions. Unfortunately they also comprise the essence of most conversations in the World of Man. A simple comment about another person or situation, for example, can evoke the whole drama of peoples' identities and problems, stirring fantasies that quickly replace the experience of Creation. Any conversation, therefore, holds the hypnotic allure of thought and fantasy. Conventional conversations challenge us to remain in the Presence and see the Divinity of the other without becoming entranced by their words and ideas.

121

Conflict: Conflict arises in the most innocent ways. Overflowing with happiness, you dance in a restaurant or give your jacket to someone in need, thus distressing friends and family who view such behavior as embarrassing or inappropriate. Distracted by beauty, you ignore an errand and fail to come home on time causing a friend or partner to worry about you. Living in the mystical consciousness of Heaven on Earth, you simply have different values and your loyalties no longer lie with the rules imposed by the World of Man. You may even respond to the suffering caused by the World of Man in ways that trigger disapproval or retaliation from authorities. Indeed, many famous mystics and saints repeatedly found themselves in trouble with the existing power structure for their enlightened behavior. These conflicts challenge us to remain in the loving patience of Presence rather than to fall back into fear and defensiveness. More importantly, the spiritual peace and kindness radiated by staying in the Presence resolve conflict more effectively than the most convincing arguments, for people find it difficult to sustain anger at a genuinely loving person.

We undertake the tremendous journey of return to Origin not to vanish into Origin or simply rest in its peace and glory but to be infused with its sacred passion and power and become so saturated with its energy and love that we can "reenter" reality and become agents with and in God of a massive transformation of all the conditions of the Creation. In other words, we are created by the Divine to participate with it in its "plan" of bringing the whole of the creation consciously into the glory of its eternal being.
Andrew Harvey (Contemporary Mystic and Author)

Slipping Back: Along the path, wants and fantasies stimulated by any residual self-concept (desires for approval, belonging, love, attractiveness, power, wealth, and importance) and the hypnosis of collective beliefs ("It's a dog-eat-dog world." "You have to fight for survival." "We're in an economic downturn.") bring even the most advanced souls back into the spell of the World of Man. Since few of us become perfectly enlightened, even those who know Heaven on Earth find themselves seduced back in the World of Man from time to time. The resulting unhappiness, of course, signals our return to delusion. Slipping back challenges us to renew our practice with Heaven's Compass and then understand how we were pulled back into the World of Man once again.

Everyday Problems: The distress associated with everyday problems often feels like an obstacle to spiritual progress because it distracts you from the peace and beauty of Heaven on Earth. With the aid of Heaven's Compass, however, everyday problems actually provide a powerful incentive for returning to Heaven on Earth. First, personal upsets remind you to use Heaven's Compass as a problem-solving resource. Then, resolving the problem – which is wonderfully reinforcing in its own right – returns you to Heaven on Earth, an even more reinforcing outcome. In this way, problems and upsets not only keep you using Heaven's Compass as a daily spiritual practice, they serve as a doorway to Heaven on Earth. When problems arise, therefore, let them be a stimulus for using Heaven's Compass. Not only will you feel better, you will make more rapid spiritual progress. (Appendix B offers detailed questions and answers, as well as practical advice, for using Heaven's Compass to resolve everyday problems and live in Heaven on Earth. In addition, you can read about the experiences of others learning to live in Heaven on Earth.)

Wisdom: Rather than representing something remembered or studied, wisdom flows directly from your first hand experience of Presence. However, since it comes from a radically different state of consciousness, you will often find others unwilling to hear this kind of wisdom when you try to share it. Moreover, such wisdom often defies conventional opinions, beliefs and values and challenges you to live its insights rather than to talk about them. Internalizing and living our wisdom also serves as a powerful stimulus for spiritual growth and maturity. Rather than relying on the opinions and approval of others, a new spiritual center matures within you, generating a capacity to function in the world with genuine maturity and independence.

The Final Step

By now, you have successfully used Heaven's Compass numerous times. You know how to experience the Presence and engage in an interesting and productive dialogue with It. If not, please keep practicing, review Appendix B or take your struggle back into Heaven's Compass to better understand it. This final step won't make much sense if you're feeling stuck. Then, when you're ready, proceed as directed below.

Heaven's Compass shows us the location of Heaven on Earth and maps the journey we must take to find it. The final instructions for entering this promised land, however, are hidden in the visionary words of Fra Giovanni cited at the beginning of this chapter. A brilliant sixteenth century Italian architect, archaeologist, scholar, and priest, Fra Giovanni wrote this as a letter to a friend at the age of 68, a time during which visions of Heaven begin to appear spontaneously to the spiritually-enlightened elder.

Fra Giovanni says we only find Heaven on Earth in the calm, peaceful and thoughtless consciousness of the present moment, and we must look for it with a vision cleansed of ugly and distorting concepts that hide Heaven's presence. We must do this until we see Heaven on Earth all around us. Then, he tells us, the final step to claiming and staying in Heaven on Earth involves courage – the courage to affirm and trust what we see rather than retreating into the shadows of skepticism and doubt.

Set your compass arrow now to Heaven on Earth and get ready to "take Heaven."

By becoming conscious, each of us becomes a builder of heaven and a redeemer of the earth. That is why this life on earth takes on an exceptional significance... there is a reversal of consciousness, a new heaven, a new earth; the physical world itself will soon change before our incredulous eyes."
Satprem (Mystic and Aurobindo Scholar)

Exercise: Take Heaven

The final barrier to finding Heaven on Earth consists of our conviction, "This can't be Heaven." In other words, when we experience the Presence but continue believing that we are not seeing Heaven on Earth, we never arrive there. This last exercise removes this deeply ingrained belief and inserts its opposite: *"This is Heaven!"* Perhaps the simplest exercise in *Finding Heaven Here*, it also requires the most courage, since those around you, and even your own conditioning, will seek to disprove it. As you proceed, remember Fra Giovanni's words, "Courage then to claim it, that is all. But courage you have."

When you are ready to proceed, remove all possible distractions, quiet your mind and say a simple prayer for enlightenment. Then, with the courage you know you have, begin. Here are your instructions:

1. Stop Thinking, Intensify Awareness and Perception in the Present, Experience the World Exactly As It Is, as if you've never seen it so clearly before, and then Come into the Presence Through Your Own Presence, that is, by becoming intensely conscious of consciousness itself.
2. Feel the Presence everywhere, pervading all space, time, and things, even you. Experience reality as conscious – a living Presence – filling the world with holiness and love.

Feel the joy of being back in this loving intimacy. Take your time. Don't rush this step. Dialogue with the Presence if it helps to intensify your experience.

3. Now say silently inside, *"This is Heaven."* Sharpen your perception even more. Say it again silently: *"This is Heaven."* Look carefully at what is around you. A third time, silently say, *"This is Heaven on Earth."* Now say these words out loud: *"This is Heaven on Earth."* Repeat the sentence again: *"This is Heaven on Earth."* Notice how your perception changes each time. Say the words one more time as you would any other incontrovertible fact and with conviction: *"THIS IS HEAVEN."* Notice how you feel. Say the words once again, this time with delight, wonder and discovery. Say them over and over again until you see it, feel it and know it as truth.

4. As your senses sharpen in Heaven's light, notice how every-thing looks so much more real, beautiful, detailed, and fresh. You should find every object examined with this naked perception fascinating, utterly new and richly bountiful in sensory qualities. Explore this fresh, new world. Blink several times to clear your vision, and then open your eyes wide to really see it. Notice what changes when you do so, how things look and feel in Heaven on Earth.

All is sacred, and we walk and talk and have our time in that which is no less than heaven.
Tony Parsons (Author)

5. Look at other people. In the light and consciousness of Heaven on Earth, notice how their faces seem to radiate light. Notice how your heart opens to them in love. Witness

the same radiance in plants and animals, in the sky and in all of Creation.

6. Focus next on something happening around you, and realize it is happening in Heaven. Ask yourself:

- How do I experience the situation differently with this realization?
- How am I moved to respond differently?
- How is everyday life transformed in the consciousness of Heaven on Earth?
- What do I want to do differently?
- How do I want to live now?

In this pure and thoughtless awareness, notice that the idea and story of "you" no longer exist; only divine Consciousness and Being exist and you are that. Notice how good it feels not to have to be anyone anymore. Feel into the Divine until you are that. Feel the divine Consciousness as your consciousness and the divine Being as your being. Know that the divine world is enough. Feel the joy of Creation.

In Heaven on Earth, divine Consciousness lives in everything. Indeed, everything is Divinity! Don't think about this; instead see Divinity everywhere. Sense its Presence and Being in everything, including "you." Ask yourself, "How do these realizations feel?"

If you have had any degree of success with this exercise, you should now be stunned, thrilled or enraptured. You've discovered a world unlike anything you ever thought. Of course! That's the whole point. When the filters of mind dissolve, you see Heaven on Earth spread out everywhere – exactly where it always has been.

What do you do with this new realization? Nothing! Don't start thinking. Don't make big plans to change your life. Don't do anything. Just experience Heaven on Earth here and now. Let life be what you find and feel in Heaven on Earth. Heaven will show you what to feel and do in every moment.

The End (and the Beginning)

Wherever you find yourself at this point let Heaven's Compass serve as your continuing guide. Bring your problems, questions, doubts, and struggles to its circular process. As you have already seen, Heaven's Compass has unlimited applications as a problem-solving method, spiritual practice and source of wisdom. It not only will guide you to Heaven on Earth, it will help you return there when the world around you seems the darkest.

How does this book end? That's up to you. You can return to the World of Man, reinstating all your customary worries, problems and goals, or you can use Heaven's Compass to keep exploring the timeless beauty of Heaven on Earth. Whatever you do, remember that the journey of Heaven's Compass remains available always, and it is never too late for *Finding Heaven Here*.

APPENDIX A

Source Material for Chapter 3: The Promise

This Appendix of Source Materials stands on its own as a resource for the reader. For easy reference, these materials are grouped in the categories presented in Chapter 3 (individual religions, mythology, archeology, naturalists, etymology, poetry, mystical experiences, ordinary experiences, and aging). In addition, I have included the complete section of text to which I referred in the book, as well as other citations not included.

Judaism

Berg, Yehuda. (2004). *The power of Kabbalah.* New York: Kahhalah Centre International.

"According to Kabbalah, there is a curtain that divides our reality into two realms, which Kabbalah identifies as the 1 percent and the 99 percent. The 1 percent realm encompasses our physical world. But this is only a tiny fraction of all Creation. It is only what we perceive with our five senses" (p. 14).

"According to the Kabbalah, the 99 percent realm is the source of all lasting fulfillment. All knowledge, wisdom, and joy dwell in this realm. This is the domain the Kabbalists call Light. Whenever we experience joy, we've made contact with this realm through some action that has taken place in the 1 percept realm" (p. 19).

"To conceal the blazing Light of the Endless World, a series of ten curtains were erected. Each successive curtain further reduced the emanation of Light, gradually transforming its brilliance almost to darkness. These ten curtains...are called the *Ten Sfirot*" (p. 78).

Genesis 28: 16-17. *The New English Bible.* (1971). New York: Oxford University Press.

"Jacob woke from his sleep and said, 'Truly the Lord is in this place, and I did not know it...This is no other than the house of God, this is the gate of heaven" (p. 31).

Levin, Faitel. (2002). *Heaven on Earth*. New York: Kehot Publication Society.

The "ultimate communion with G-d" takes place here, "Not by releasing some hidden meaning and significance latent in the physical, not by achieving the religious feat of sublimating the physical, but rather in relating to G-d as found in the physical itself – precisely in the absence of spiritual meaning and significance, specifically because it is physical and not sublime" (p. 23).

"It is specifically here that G-d desired a *dirah*, a dwelling place. No need to transcend this world! It is here, here as nowhere else, that the human can fulfill his true spiritual potential, it is specifically here that the deepest recesses of the Divine can be reached" (p. 32).

"...this reality is transparent to its true being – the *essence* of this reality is nothing but the Essence of G-d" (p. 52).

"It is specifically in this world, in performing very human, very bodily good deeds that the essence of G-d is reached. This world is not an antechamber: it is the palace itself" (p. 125).

Levin, Michael. (2002). *The complete idiot's guide to Jewish spirituality and mysticism*. New York: Alpha (Penguin Group, Inc.).

"Rabbi Shneur Zalman was the founder of Chabad, or Lubavitch Hasidus, perhaps the best-known branch of the Hasidic world known to secular and orthodox Jews...The purpose of living according to Jewish law and custom, Zalman writes, is not just to attain heaven, but to achieve a taste of heaven on Earth. It is possible, Zalman claims, through perfection of one's character and through proper adherence to Jewish law and custom, to experience a taste of the bliss that awaits us in the afterlife" (pp. 133-4).

"If you take the first four letters of *pshat, remez, drash*, and *sod*...(the four levels of Biblical interpretation) and throw in vowel sounds to create a word, you get the Hebrew word *pardes*, or garden, from which we derive the English word 'paradise.' In other words, when we truly devote ourselves to understanding Biblical texts or other aspects of Jewish law and lore, we don't just attain wisdom and knowledge. We attain paradise. Jews believe the key to paradise is study" (p. 47).

Matt, Daniel. (1996). *The essential Kabbalah*. San Francisco: Harper.

"The kabbalists made the fantastic claim that their mystical teachings derived from the Garden of Eden. This suggests that Kabbalah conveys our original nature: the unbounded awareness of Adam and Eve. We have lost this nature, the most ancient tradition, as the inevitable consequence of tasting the fruit of knowledge, the price of maturity and culture. The kabbalist yearns to recover that primordial tradition, to regain cosmic consciousness, without renouncing the world. The Garden of Eden, they say, is constantly flowing into our world" (p. 2).

"When powerful light is concealed and clothed in a garment, it is revealed. Though concealed, the light is actually revealed, for were it not concealed, it could not be revealed. This is like wishing to gaze at the dazzling sun. Its dazzle conceals it, for you cannot look at its overwhelming brilliance. Yet when you conceal it – looking at it through screens – you can see and not be harmed. So it is with emanation (of Heaven's light): by concealing and clothing itself, it reveals itself..." (p. 91).

"The secret of fulfilling the mitsvot (commandment) is the mending of all the worlds and drawing forth the emanation from above...It is up to us to actualize the divine potential in the world" (pp. 1-2).

Sheinkin, David. (1986). *Path of the Kaballah*. New York: Paragon House.

"Kabbalists have taught for centuries that the spiritual world is right in front of us – in fact, it surrounds our every step" (p. 98).

Van Scott, Miriam. (1998). *Encyclopedia of heaven*. New York: St. Martin's Press.

"In the second century before Christ, new ideas about a Last Judgment and a system of final rewards began to spread. This crystallized into the concept of GAN EDEN, the paradise created for Adam and Eve before they sinned against God and were banished, now restored to its original splendor. Souls of the faithful who had led moral lives could look forward to enjoying eternity in this garden, which would be located on earth after the end of the world" (pp. 152-3).

Weinberg, Noah. (n.d.). *Shabbat – Heaven on Earth*. Retrieved August 22, 2006, from http://www.aish.com/literacy/mitzvahs/Shabbat_-_Heaven_on_Earth.asp.

"Shabbat is the name for the seventh day of the week. The Torah tells us, 'Six days you shall work, and the seventh day is Shabbat, for the Lord your God."

"The midrash says: When the Jewish people were gathered at Mount Sinai to receive the Torah, God told them that Heaven would be their reward for keeping the commandments. The Jews asked God, 'How do we know that Heaven is so great? How about a free sample to see if it's worthwhile?...God wasn't upset. He knew that Heaven is where we experience the pure and unadulterated pleasure of the infinite God. So He said, 'No problem. I'll send you a sample. Shabbat.' Thus the Sages say: Shabbat is 'a taste of Heaven on Earth.' If Heaven is pure spirituality, then Shabbat is a taste of that experience."

"...the primary goal of Shabbat: getting in touch with God...On Shabbat, the spiritual level of the world is intensified. God immerses us in a spiritual environment, and our perception of His closeness is heightened...Shabbat is the period of time in which God's presence is felt more intensely than any other time during the week."

Christianity

Bankcroft, Anne. (1982). *The luminous vision*. London: Unwin Hyman Limited.

"To surrender to things as they are, in their isness, is to love them as they are; to love them as they are is to be at one with them...By becoming awakened to the isness of creation, we find ourselves in Nirvana – or Heaven – fulfilled to running over, and wonderfully in accord with all beings – human, animal or mere substance" (p. 175).

Blake, William. Quoted in *The portable Blake*. (1976) Alfred Kazin. (Ed.). New York: Penguin Books.

"If the doors of perception were cleansed everything would appear to man as it is, infinite" (p. 258).

Boehm, Jacob. *Dialogues on the supersensual life.* (undated). Law, William, Trans. Montana: Kessinger Publishing Company.

"Heaven is throughout the whole World, and it is also without the World over all, even everywhere that is, or that can be even so much as imagined. It filleth all, it is within all, it is without all, it encompasseth all; without division (p. 98).

"Wheresoever thou findest God manifesting himself in Love, there thou findest Heaven, without traveling for it so much as one foot" (p. 83).

"Men seek and find not, because they seek it not in the naked Ground where it lieth; but in something or other where it never will be, nor can be. They seek it in their own *Will*, and they find it not. They seek it in their *Self-Desire*, and they meet not with it. They look for it in an *Image*, or in an *Opinion*, or in *Affection*,....and so they miss of what they seek, for want of diving into the Supernatural and Supersensual Ground, where the Treasure is hid" (p. 75).

Campbell, Joseph. (1988) *The power of myth*. New York: DoubleDay.

"This is Eden. When you see the kingdom spread upon the earth, the old way of living in the world is annihilated. That is the end of the world. The end of the world is not an event to come, it is an event of psychological transformation, of visionary transformation. You see not the world of solid things but a world of radiance" (p. 230).

"Eternity isn't some later time. Eternity isn't even a long time. Eternity has nothing to do with time. Eternity is that dimension of here and now that all thinking in temporal terms cuts off. And if you don't get it here, you won't get it anywhere...This is it" (p. 67).

"The difference between everyday living and living in those moments of ecstasy is the difference between being outside and inside the Garden" (p. 107).

Cardenal, Ernesto. (1995) *Abide in love*. New York: Orbis Books.

"Union with God makes the earth a paradise once more. Where God is with me, there is paradise and the whole of nature is the lovely background to our friendship...For those who live in union with God all things are transfigured by a special light, and joy springs from them - even the most common everyday things. Blessedness falls on every moment of their life and there is a kind of enchantment upon everything they touch, everything they do" (p. 138).

Cayce, Edgar. (2004). *In a waking state*. Virginia Beach, VA: A.R.E. Press.

"Then where is heaven? Where is God? In Him we live and move and have our being. Then *in* us, *about* us, *over* us, *under* us – all about us – is heaven" (p. 208).

"That which would prevent our knowing where heaven is, is

in ourselves only" (p. 209).

"All of heaven and earth is made up of and from one Force or Source. Man, then, left heaven or is in heaven according to what he does *with* that Force, making for himself a heaven or a hell, or an earth, or some other place of experience" (p. 211).

Chittister, Joan. (1999). *In search of belief.* Miguori, Missouri: Liguori/Triumph.

"...heaven already exists...heaven is already here...Heaven is the state of perfect immersion into God,..." (p. 49).

"If I do not burst into heaven here, make heaven here for me, for everyone, I sincerely doubt that I will find it anywhere else" (p. 51).

"Am I 'going to heaven'? No, I am already there and it is getting more heavenly every day" (p. 52).

Eckhart, Meister, in Fox, Mathew. (1980). *Breakthrough: Meister Eckhart's Creation Spirituality in new translation.* New York: Doubleday.

"An equally false consciousness is established, Eckhart believes, by imagining that heaven is something that begins after this life. Eternal life is now for Eckhart, and if heaven has not already begun for us it is our dualistic way of envisioning our lives that is the major obstacle..." (p. 44-45).

"The kingdom is here when we are awake enough to see it. For Eckhart, the coming of the kingdom depends upon our consciousness" (p. 142).

"Eckhart is so taken with this promise of eternal life before death that he dismisses speculation about life after death. What we shall be hereafter is not yet revealed, he rightly points out. So why waste one's energy getting to heaven when heaven has already arrived" (p. 334).

Fox, Matthew. (1983). *Original blessing*. Santa Fe: Bear and Company.

"The creation-centered spiritual tradition...rejects the dualism of heaven/earth...(Fox, 1983, p. 105).

"Realized eschatology is the experience that Now is the time; Now is the place;...Now is the moment of divine break-through...Therefore heaven has already burst forth into human and cosmic times..." (p. 105)

Fox, Mathew. (1995). *Wrestling with the prophets*. New York: Jeremy Tarcher/Putnam.

"That is what Jesus is trying to tell us: the kingdom is already here, it is among us! In the Western theological tradition, this is called 'realized eschatology'" (p. 139).

Goldsmith, Joel. (1993). *Conscious union with God*. New Jersey: Carol Publishing Group.

"Heaven and earth are not two places; heaven and earth are one and the same: Earth is our mortal concept of heaven, and heaven is our real awareness of the earth. In other words, heaven is earth correctly understood" (p. 88).

Griffiths, Bede. (1976). *Return to the center*. Springfield: Templegate Publishers.

"This is the essential message of all religion. The infinite, transcendent, holy Mystery, which is what is signified by 'God' or 'Heaven', is present in the world...The Kingdom is universal...It has existed from the beginning, in all times and in all places" (pp. 107-8).

Griffiths, Bede. *A new vision of reality*. In Harvey, Andrew. (1996). San Francisco: HarperCollins.

"This earth and all that is in it, and the whole cosmic order to which it belongs, has to undergo a transformation; it has to become a "new heaven and a new earth."...This is the ultimate goal of human history and of the created universe....Our present world is conditioned by our present mode of consciousness; only when that consciousness passes from its present dualistic mode conditioned by time and space will the new creation appear..." (214-15).

Harvey, Andrew. (1996). *The essential mystics: The soul's journey into truth.* San Francisco: HarperCollins.

"We all long for heaven where God is, but we have it in our power to be in heaven with Him at this very moment" (p. 214).

Harvey, Andrew (2000). *The direct path.* New York: Broadway Books.

"Jesus' 'Kingdom' and Aurobindo's 'Supramental Creation' are not in any way otherworldly utopian dreams; they represent the final possibilities of the evolution of the human species, the ultimate flowering of human potential...a wholly new world is waiting to be engendered....This is the kingdom of heaven on earth that all the Mother-Father's lovers see clearly in their illumined eye of contemplation; this is the new world that they all know is not a dream and not a fantasy but wholly possible...The Garden of Eden does not lie in our mythical past but in our potential future" (pp. 60-1).

Holmes, Ernest. (1997). *The science of mind.* New York: Jeremy P. Tarcher/Putnam.

"Heaven is within, it revolves around us; it is the result of that atmosphere of conviction which our thought awakens within us. The Kingdom of Heaven is unformed, unlimited, uncondi-tioned...It is the real state of Being. We do not *make* it real, for it is eternal Reality. If we abide in the Father and He abides in us...our Kingdom of Heaven is a good *place* in which to live" (p. 598).

Jesus. In Meyer, Marvin. (1992). *Gospel of Thomas*. San Francisco: HarperSanFrancisco.

"...the kingdom is inside you and it is outside you" (p. 23).

"What you look for has come, but you do not know it" (p. 43).

"...the father's kingdom is spread out upon the earth, and people do not see it" (p. 65).

Johnson, Robert. (1998). *Balancing heaven and earth*. San Francisco: HarperCollins.

"If one works faithfully and patiently at this task of balancing heaven and earth, eventually one may even realize something more remarkable: that the two worlds are in fact one" (p. xii).

"The accomplishment of my life has been to find some synthesis, to learn that heaven (and hell) is not some other time or place but right here, right now..." (p. 15).

Keck, Robert. (2000). *Sacred quest*. West Chester, PA: Chrysalis Books.

"Humanity collectively, it appears, has been on a maturational journey akin to that of an individual: growing through childhood epoch, then an adolescent epoch, and now entering an adult epoch...into a more mature set of values wherein spiritual maturation became the central evolutionary task" (xix-xx).

"Heaven and earth are one. Human and divine are one. Eternity is available for us right now, right here, spread throughout the earth, inside us, and all around us. We need simply to awaken...to the ever-present heaven, the eternal now" (pp 265-6).

Kelsey, Morton. (1979). *Afterlife: The other side of dying*. New York: Paulist Press.

"The central message of Jesus of Nazareth is about heaven. To the people who heard him it was an amazing message...They knew about hoping for heaven in the future and trying their best to earn it and avoid punishment. But Jesus spoke about finding heaven within and around and among us, as well as in a future that is hidden from us...Heaven, Jesus taught, can be shared in the here and now" (p. 157).

"...Jesus was speaking about a heaven which is both now and hereafter, both immanent and transcendent" (p. 158).

"...Jesus clearly suggested that the kingdom of God is available now, as well as in eternity" (p. 168).

Lewis, C.S. (1974). *The great divorce.* New York: Macmillan Publishing Company.

"But what, you ask, of earth? Earth, I think, will not be found by anyone to be in the end a very distinct place. I think earth, if chosen instead of Heaven, will turn out to have been, all along, only a region of Hell: and earth, if put second to.Heaven, to have been from the beginning a part of Heaven itself" (p. 11).

"...it will be true for those who have completed the journey (and for no others) to say that good is everything and Heaven everywhere" (p. 10).

Luke: 20-21 *The New English Bible.* (1971). New York: Oxford Univ. Press.

"The Pharisees asked him, 'When will the kingdom come?' He said, 'You cannot tell by observation when the kingdom of God comes. There is no saying, 'Look, here it is!' or 'there it is!'; for in fact the kingdom of God is among you.'" (footnote on alternative translations: "*Or* for in fact the kingdom of God is within you, *or* for in fact the kingdom of God is within your grasp, *or* for suddenly the kingdom of God will be among you.") (p. 98).

McDannell, Colleen and Lang, Bernhard. (1990). *Heaven: A history.* New York: Vintage Books.

"There is a long tradition in Christian history which acknowl-edges that glimpses of heaven can be experienced on earth: in the quiet of meditation, the beauty of the cathedral, the drama of the Mass, or the fellowship of Christian community. Friedrich Schleiermacher, when confronted with death, found consolation not in the expectation of a future life but in the experience of the divine in the present. Schleiermacher maintained that the Christian should strive to increase those glimpses of heaven on earth, rather than becoming preoccupied with life after death...Schleiermacher summarized his creed by saying that 'in the midst of finitude to be one with the Infinite and in every moment to be eternal is the immortality of religion.'...Schleiermacher warned his fellow Christians, 'and weep if you are swept along in the stream of time without carrying heaven within you' - that is, in every moment of this life" (pp. 332-3).

Myss, Caroline. (2007, February). Andrew Harvey Interviews Caroline Myss on St. Terewsa of Avila. *Andrew Harvey*. Retrieved 2/28/07 from http://www.infor@andrewharvey.net.

"So I have this intuition in my bones that says, 'Heaven walks next to you.' Not above you, within and next to...What would happen, for example, if I shifted the location of my idea of God and decided that the Divine did not exist in some sort of cosmic distance above or beyond...That shift in compass would mean the end of all boundaries between this physical world and a Divine world as the two would merge into one."

Paul, Pope John II. (1999, August 7). *The Sacramento Bee.*

Heaven is "neither an abstraction nor a physical place in the clouds, but a living and personal relationship of union with the Holy Trinity."

"Hell is not a punishment imposed externally by God, but the condition resulting from attitudes and actions which people adopt in this life...Hell exists, not as a place but as a state, a way of being of the person who suffers the pain of the deprivation of God."

Robertson, Pat. (1982). *The secret kingdom*. New York: Thomas Nelson Publishers.

"Yes, the kingdom of God is here – now. And the message of the Bible is that we can and should look from this visible world, which is finite, into the invisible world, which is infinite...We should do more than look, however, if we believe the Scriptures. We should enter" (p. 37).

Sanford, John. In Kelsey, Morton. (1979). *Afterlife: The other side of dying*. New York: Paulist Press.

"The kingdom of God is a non-physical reality, a personal state of being, an archetypal spiritual realm...It is a mystical reality in that only an *experience* with the kingdom can reveal what it is...The kingdom is an objective reality because it is not subjectively created by man's experience or wishes, any more than a man who has seen the Himalayas for the first time can say that he has created them" (p. 161).

"All of this describes the kingdom as a present spiritual reality, but the kingdom as a spiritual reality also has an eschatological character. It is a present state insofar as it is a reality which already exists within men, and in which those men can participate who are conscious enough and have formed their lives according its pattern. But the kingdom in another sense is still to come in the future for it cannot be said to be completely established until all men belong to it" (p. 162).

Steindl-Rast, David. In Elliot, William. (1995). *Tying rocks to clouds*. New York: Doubleday.

"I believe in heaven! But I don't believe in heaven as a place somewhere else. Heaven is everything transfigured by God's presence. Therefore, for many people heaven starts here, and for many people, hell starts here" (p. 248).

"We have all experienced heaven and hell. In our best moments, in what Abraham Maslow calls the 'peak experience,' we have experienced heaven...we are really there, and this is *now*. That is where we experience heaven" (p. 248).

Tolle, Eckhart. (2005). *A new Earth*. New York: Penguin Group.

"We need to understand here that heaven is not a location but refers to the inner realm of consciousness. This is the esoteric meaning of the word, and this is also its meaning in the teachings of Jesus. Earth, on the other hand, is the outer manifestation in form, which is always a reflection of the inner. Collective human consciousness and life on our planet are intrinsically connected. *'A new heaven' is the emergence of a transformed state of human consciousness, and 'a new earth' is its reflection in the physical realm"* (p. 23).

"...awakening is the realization of Presence. So the new heaven, the awakened consciousness, is not a future state to be achieved. A new heaven and a new earth are arising within you at this moment, and if they are not arising at this moment, they are no more than a thought in your head and therefore not arising at all" (p. 308).

Traherne, Thomas. (1960) *Centuries*. New York: Harper Brothers.

"Your enjoyment of the world is never right, till every morning you awake in Heaven; see yourself in your Father's Palace; and look upon the skies, the earth, and the air as Celestial Joys...the world is a mirror of infinite beauty, yet no man sees it. It is a Temple of Majesty, yet no man regards. It is a region of Light and Peace, did not men disquiet it. It is the Paradise of God" (pp. 14-15).

"The dust and stones of the street were as precious as gold...The green trees when I saw them first through one of the gates transported and ravished me, their sweetness and unusual beauty made my heart to leap, and almost mad with ecstasy, they were such strange and wonderful things. The Men! O what venerable and reverend creatures did the aged seem! Immortal

Cherubim! And young men glittering and sparkling Angels, and maids strange seraphic pieces of life and beauty! Boys and girls tumbling in the street, and playing, were moving jewels...all things abided eternally as they were in their proper places. Eternity was manifest in the Light of the Day, and something infinite behind everything appeared...The city seemed to stand in Eden, or to be built in Heaven" (p. 110).

Hinduism

Maharishi, Maresh. (n.d.) *Creating Heaven on Earth*. Retrieved August 22, 2006, from http://www.alltm.org/

"Heaven on Earth has been the most laudable aspiration of the wise throughout the ages. Creation of Heaven on Earth is the most desirable project in the entire history of the human race. Marharishi's programs to create Heaven on Earth contain practical, simple, scientifically-proven, time-tested knowledge that can bring Heaven on Earth to any society."

Maharshi, Ramana. (1984). *Talks with Sri Ramana Mararshi*. Tiruvannamalai: Sri Ramanasramam.

"This is the Kingdom of Heaven. The Kingdom of Heaven mentioned in the Bible and this world are not two different regions. 'The Kingdom is within you,' says the Bible. So it is. The realized being sees this as the Kingdom of Heaven whereas the others see it as 'this world'" (p. 565).

Muktananda. In Star, Jonathan. (Ed.). (1991). *Two suns rising*. New York: Bantam Books.

"This world is the beautiful Garden of Shiva, of the Lord, made so that you can walk in it with great joy" (p. 221).

Yogananda, Paramhansa. In Walters, Donald. (1990) *The essence of self-realization*. Nevada City: Crystal Clarity.

"Heaven and hell are realities even here on earth..." (p. 65).

"Heaven is not 'up there,' as people commonly imagine. It is all around us. It is just behind our physical vision. I see it all the time, and I spend much of my time there. It is a vast universe, composed of beautiful lights, sounds, and colors. The colors of the material plane are very dull by comparison. Heaven's beauty is like the most radiant sunset you have ever seen, and even more beautiful" (pp. 74-75).

Buddhism

Mipham, Sakyong. (2005). What do you see when you're awake? *Parabola*, Vol 30, (1), p. 59.

"When we're awake, we see that we are and always have been complete and perfect beings in a complete and perfect world...When we're awake, we see the inherent and perpetual radiance of the world."

Sheng-yen. (1997). *Complete enlightenment*. Elmhurst, NY: Dharma Drum Publications.

"The Pure Lands mentioned in the sutra include the world we inhabit now. Buddhas and bodhisattvas view this world as a Pure Land. Ordinary sentient beings are unable to see it as such because they cannot overcome their addictions to negative patterns of self-attachment and discover this intrinsic samadhi. On the other hand, practitioners who enter the door of Ch'an would not view the world as impure, miserable, or chaotic. To them it would be a beautiful place. People who reach this level of their practice recognize beauty in everything" (p. 81).

Sogyal Rinpoche (1992). *The Tibetan book of living and dying*. San Francisco: Harper.

"Everything that we see around us is seen as it is because we have been repeatedly solidifying our experience of inner and outer reality in the same way, lifetime after lifetime, and this has led to the mistaken assumption that what we see is objectively real. In fact, as we go further along the spiritual path, we learn how to work directly with our fixed perceptions. All our old concepts of the world or matter or even ourselves are purified and dissolved, and an entirely new, what you could call 'heavenly' field of vision and perception opens up" (p. 115).

Suzuki., D.T. In Berstein, Andrew. (1996). *Swedenborg: Buddha of the north.* Penn: Swedenborg Foundation.

"In the summer of 1954, while meeting with religion scholars Henry Corbin and Mircea Eliade, D.T. Suzuki was asked what resemblances he found between Mahayana Buddhism and the theology of Emanuel Swedenborg. According to Corbin, Suzuki suddenly brandished a spoon and declared, 'This spoon *now* exists in Paradise...We are *now* in Heaven'" (p. xv).

Thich Nhat Hanh. (1999). *Going home.* New York: Penguin Putnam.

"Here is the Pure Land, the Pure Land is here" (p. 52).

"You don't have to die in order to enter the Kingdom of God. It is better to do it now when you are fully alive. In fact, you can do it only when you are fully alive...the Kingdom doesn't have to come and you do not have to go to it; it is already here" (p. 103).

"The Kingdom of God...is not situated in space and time. You do not have to die in order to enter the Kingdom of God; in fact you are already in it now and here. The only thing is that you don't know that" (p. 155).

"...you can enjoy being there in the Kingdom of God twenty-four hours a day" (p. 157).

Thich Nhat Hanh. (2002). *No death, no fear.* New York: The Berkley Publishing Group.

"We also do not have to die in order to enter the kingdom of God. The kingdom of God is our very foundation here and now" (p. 107).

"The Pure Land is not somewhere else; it is right here, in the present. It is in every cell of our bodies...There is not one day when I do not walk in the kingdom of God" (pp. 108-9).

Thich Nhat Hanh. (2003). *Finding our true home.* Berkeley: Parallax Press.

"The Kingdom of God is not somewhere else. Jesus was firmly established in the Kingdom of God in the present moment. To follow in his footsteps, disciples of Jesus must realize the kingdom of God in the here and the now. To wait until after we die to enter paradise is a shame. Already the beautiful path awaits us; the path of compassion, understanding, and peace is right below our feet. We need only take one step in mindfulness and all the beauties of the Kingdom of God will be available for us to enjoy and to benefit from" (p. 85).

Yuansou. (1989) In Cleary, Thomas. (1989) *Zen essence.* Boston: Shambhala.

"The mountains, rivers, earth, grasses, trees, and forests, are always emanating a subtle, precious light, day and night, always emanating a subtle, precious sound, demonstrating and expounding to all people the unsurpassed ultimate truth" (p. 76).

Yung-Chia. In Star, Johathan. (Ed.). (1991)*Two suns rising.* New York: Bantam Books.

"The Gate of Heaven is wide open with not a single obstruction before it" (p. 72).

Islam (including Sufism)
Chittick, William. (1989) *The Sufi path of knowledge.* New York: State University of New York Press.

Speaking of the ninety-nine names of God, Chittick quotes al-'Arabi, "If the servant counts those names, he enters the Garden" (p. 369).

Chittick states elsewhere, "Simply put, useful knowledge leads to deliverance...which is none other than happiness or 'felicity'...felicity is to attain, in his actual situation...it is to enter the Garden by becoming a locus of manifestation for the divine names of gentleness and beauty" (p. 150).

The perfectly realized man, al-'Arabi adds, also witnesses the divine, "...in the heaven of this world" (p. 379).

Firdausi. In Star, Johathan. (Ed.). (1991) *Two suns rising*. New York: Bantam Books.

If on earth there be
  a Paradise of Bliss,
It is this,
It is this,
It is this (p. 145)

Hafiz. In Landinsky, Daniel. (1999) *The gift*. New York: Penguin Putnum Inc.

The mule I sit on while I recite
Stares off in one direction
But then gets drunk.
And lost in
Heaven (p. 133).

Al-'Arabi, in Helminski, Kabir. (2000). *The knowing heart*. Boston: Shambhala.

"This world is not bad; on the contrary, it is the field of eternity. What you plant here you will reap there. This world is the way to eternal bliss and good, worthy to be cherished and worthy to be praised" (p. 236).

Helminski, Kabir. (2000). *The knowing heart*. Boston: Shambhala.

Sufi aphorism: "When we stop complaining, we will be in paradise" (p. 263).

Kabir. In Bly, Robert. (1977). *The Kabir book*. Boston: Beacon Press.
  The idea that the soul will join with the ecstatic
  just because the body is rotten –
  that is all fantasy.
  What is found now is found then (p. 24).

Khayyam, Omar. In Yogananda, Paramhansa. (1994). *The Rubaiyat of Omar Khayyam explained*. Nevada City, CA: Crystal Clarity Publishers.
  Here with a Loaf of Bread beneath the Bough,
  A Flask of Wine, a Book of Verse – and Thou
  Beside me singing in the Wilderness –
  And Wilderness is Paradise now (p. 48).

Rumi. (1984). In Moyne, John & Barks, Coleman. (1984) *Open secret*. Vermont: Threshold Books.
  The breeze at dawn has secrets to tell you.
  Don't go back to sleep.
  You must ask for what you really want.
  Don't go back to sleep.
  People are going back and forth across the doorsill
  Where the two worlds touch.
  The door is wide and open.
  Don't go back to sleep (p. 7).

Rumi. In Harvey, Andrew. (Ed.). (1996). *The essential mystics*. New York: HarperCollins.
  No Heaven or earth, just this mysterious place
  We walk in dazedly, where being here
  Or there, in time or not, are only
  Two motions of the same ecstatic breathing" (p. 161).

Rumi. In Abdulla, Raficq. (Ed.). (2006). *Words of paradise*. New York: Barnes and Noble.

Where you dwell is dear to my sight
A celestial city bedecked in light.
In whatever corner you are found
Small as a needle's eye, is holy ground.
Wherever the rainbow of your face alights
Be it the dank gorge of a well, it's paradise.
With your presence in hell a heaven is discerned
The rigour of prison to a lover's garden is turned.
The Devil's chamber with you glows with delight,
Your absence makes beauty horror, widowing my sight
(p. 25).

Taoism

Armstrong, Karen. (2006). *The great transformation*. New York: Alfred A. Knopf.

In this history of world religions, Karen Armstrong points out that the ancient Chinese philosophers did not split Heaven and Earth; rather they developed rituals to experience their unity. She explains,

"Like most other religious systems at this time (ninth century BCE), that of the Chinese was preoccupied with preserving the natural order of the universe by rituals *(li)*, which would ensure that human society conformed to the Way *(dao)* of Heaven….there was no ontological separation between Heaven and Earth" (p. 70).

"Without the work of human beings, Heaven could not act. Ordinary earthly actions were therefore sacramental, sacred activities, which enabled people to share in a divine process…Instead of seeing a gulf between Heaven and Earth, the Chinese saw only a continuum" (p. 71).

"By the ninth century (BCE) they had begun to appreciate that the transformative effect of ritual was far more important than the manipulation of the gods...The ritual gave the participants a vision of harmony, beauty, and sacredness that stayed with them when they returned to the confusion of their ordinary lives...By submitting to the minute details of the liturgy, they gave themselves up to the larger pattern, and created – at least for a time – a holy community, where past and present, Heaven and Earth were one" (p. 76).

Lao Tzu. In Bynner, Witter. (1944).*The way of life according to Lao Tzu*. New York: Perigee Books.

> Before creation a presence existed,
> Self-contained, complete,
> Formless, voiceless, mateless,
> Changeless,
> Which yet pervaded itself
> With unending motherhood...
>
> In this sense
> The way of life is fulfilled,
> Heaven is fulfilled,
> Earth fulfilled
> And a fit man also is fulfilled...(Verse 25, p. 55).

Li Po. In Bly, Robert. (1995) *The soul is here for its own joy*. New Jersey: Ecco Press.

> If you were to ask me why I dwell among green mountains,
> I should laugh silently; my soul is serene.
> The peach blossom follows the moving water;
> There is another heaven and earth beyond the world of men

(p. 247).

Takakusu. In Jacobs, Alan (Ed). (1997). *The element book of mystical verse*. Rockport MA., Element Books.

> The Perfect Way is only difficult for those who pick and

choose;

Do not like, do not dislike, all will then be clear.

Make a hairbreadth difference, and Heaven and Earth are set apart (p. 36).

Native American Spirituality

Deloria, Vine. (1994). *God is red*. Golden, CO: Fulcrum Publishing.

"In the western tradition, revelation has generally been interpreted as the communication to human beings of a divine plan...American Indians and other tribal peoples did not take this path in interpreting revelations and religious experiences. The structure of their religious traditions is taken directly from the world around them, from their relationships with other forms of life...Hence revelation was seen as a continuous process of adjustment to the natural surroundings and not as a specific message valid for all times and places" (pp. 66-7).

Ladkin, Donna. (Ed.). *Native American Spirituality*. Retrieved December 30, 2004.

http://www.greenspirit.org.uk/resources/NatAmerSpirit.html

"Above all else, Native American spirituality is a land-based spirituality. The relationship between the land and the people was one of mystical inter-dependence."

"Critically, as opposed to those of us who grew up in the Western Christian tradition, the Native American experienced Earth as HOME. The Earth is perfectly adapted to all of our requirements as human beings. The implications of this are huge in the way in which the Native American treated the Earth from day to day. First of all, the 'Kingdom of Heaven' is actually happening here and now, not in some mythical place in the future."

Seattle, Chief. In Mitchell, Stephen (Ed.). *The enlightened mind.*
New York: HarperCollins Publishers.

"Every part of this earth is sacred to my people. Every hillside,
every valley, every clearing and wood, is holy in the memory and
experience of my people" (p. 176).

Teasdale, Wayne. (2001). *The mystic heart.* Novato, Ca: The New
World Library.

"The outer path...embraces the natural world as a manifestation of the divine glory in, behind, and surrounding it. This
commitment is the basis of Native American spirituality. Indeed,
in all the indigenous cultures of the world, nature is utterly
central to their experience of ultimate realty...The natural world
provides an external medium through which we may seek and
encounter the divine, and through it the divine also seeks contact
with us...The experience of the divine in the natural world is a
defining realization for all peoples whose life is surrounded by
nature" (pp. 87-88).

"The relationship of indigenous peoples to the earth is
mystical – the basis of their culture, life, and spirituality...the
earth itself is their church..." (p. 185).

Mythology

Ashton, John and Whyte, Tom. (2001) *The quest for paradise.* San
Francisco: Harper.

Aston and Whyte review numerous myths and legends from
around the world recalling a Golden Age, now lost, when Heaven
and Earth were still connected or unified. But these tales also hint
that pockets of this unity still existed on earth reachable only by
heroic, consciousness changing journeys. Here is one such tale
from the Celtic tradition.

"The *Voyage of Bran* is one of the earliest examples of the
common Celtic genre of *immrama*, a term used to refer to stories of
ocean voyages crammed with wonderful events and ending up in

fairyland...Bran...falls asleep one evening while listening to the sound of mysterious music. On waking he finds lying beside him a silver branch covered with white blossoms. The next day he receives a mysterious visitor, a woman who sings to him and his men of the glory and beauty of a land over the ocean to the west of Erin, an island supported by four golden pillars full of all kinds of delights...There is no pain on this island, no sickness, no sorrow, no death...Bran then sails off with his companions, and after many adventures, arrives at the Island of Joy. Leaving one of his men behind, he proceeds with the others to the Isle of Women...They are treated to wonderful feasts in which all the food and drink has the taste that each of them most desires; and they stay so long that they lose all sense of time" (p. 27).

Heinberg, Richard. (1989). *Memories and visions of paradise.* Los Angeles: Jeremy Tarcher.

"...the image of a vanished Paradise and the quest for its restoration are staple themes in world folklore. Nearly all ancient peoples had traditions of a primordial era when humanity lived a simple yet magical existence in attunement with Nature. The ancients said that this original Golden Age came to an end because of some tragic mistake or failure that forced a separation between Heaven and Earth. Further, they said that the rupture between the two worlds precipitated a descent into the separateness, fear, and greed that characterize human nature as we know it today" (p. xxvi).

"Paradise is not just the stuff of mythic memories. People of virtually every civilization and tribal culture, in every era, have nourished dreams of a golden world to come...Prophets of every spiritual tradition have envisioned an eventual dramatic end to the present human state and a general renewal of the world - a return of the original Paradise" (p. 115).

"The essence of Paradise is, as we have seen, equivalent to what various traditions have termed nirvana, ecstasy, divine union, and cosmic consciousness" (p. 254).

"Perhaps, if we are willing to become partners once again with Heaven and Nature in the realization of an already existing design that transcends self-centered human purpose, then memory and vision may converge in a realized Paradise" (p. 256).

Scafi, Alessandro. (2006). *Mapping paradise*. Chicago: The University of Chicago Press.

"Throughout history, humans have searched for paradise. When early Christians adopted the Hebrew Bible, and with it the story of Genesis, the Garden of Eden became an idyllic habitat for all mankind. Medieval Christians believed paradise was a place on earth, different from the world, yet part of it, situated in real geography and indicated on maps. From the Renaissance through to the Enlightenment, the mapping of paradise validated the authority of Holy Scripture and supported Christian faith. But from the early nineteenth century onwards, the question of the exact location of paradise was left not to theologians but to laymen. And at the beginning of the twenty-first century, there is still no end of the stream of theories on the exact position of the mythical Garden of Eden" (front dust cover).

Archeology

Baring, Anne & Cashford, Jules. (1993). *The myth of the goddess: Evolution of an image*. London: Arkana (Penguin Group).

"The Mother Goddess, wherever she is found, is an image that inspires and focuses a perception of the universe as an organic, alive and sacred whole, in which humanity, the Earth and all life on Earth participate as 'her children'. Everything is woven together in one cosmic web, where all orders of manifest and unmanifest life are related, because all share in the sanctity of the original source...the Earth and all creation were of the same substance as the Goddess. Earth was her epiphany: the divine was immanent as creation" (p. xi).

Naturalists

Burroughs, John. In Maggio, Rosalie. (1997). *The journey inward.* New York: Barnes & Noble.

"One of the hardest lessons we have to learn in this life, and one that many persons never learn, is to see the divine, the celestial, the pure in the common, the near at hand – to see that heaven lies about us in this world" (p. 76).

Findhorn Community. (1975). *The Findhorn garden.* New York: HarperCollins Publishers.

Gardeners, like naturalists, work directly with nature to learn the practical secrets for cultivating plant life. Some, like the founders of the Findhorn Community in Scotland, believed they had discovered ways of communicating directly with the spiritual energy and intelligence of plants to bring forth Heaven on Earth.

"Man is learning how to be a gardener on all levels, a co-creator with God, a re-creator of the Earth...This is the promise of recreating the Garden that is Earth's essence" (p. 147).

"God, the devas and the nature spirits are all aspects of one life, the same life we are expressing. They are, in fact, within us, and each of us has the power to work with these forces to create Heaven on Earth" (p. 152).

One man in the Findhorn Community, recounting his experience of Heaven on Earth in a London park, described, "I followed the path until I came to the Rhododendron Walk...At its entrance is a huge cedar tree...I sat there for some time...then rose...As I did so, I felt a great build-up of power and a vast increase in awareness. Colors and forms became more significant. I was aware of every single leaf on the bushes and trees, of every blade of grass on the path standing out with startling clarity. It was as if physical reality had become much more real than it normally is, and the three-dimensional effect we are used to had become more solid...I had the impression of complete reality, and all that lies within and beyond it felt immediately imminent. There was an acute feeling of being one with nature in a complete way, as well as being one with the Divine, which produced great exultation, and a deep sense of awe and wonder." He concluded, "Because of our dulled senses and our habit of going through life wearing materialistic blinders in a condition verging on sleep-walking, we are unaware of the fantastic beauty of the life around us" (pp. 118-9).

Laski, Marghanita. (1961). *Ecstasy in secular and religious experiences*. Los Angeles: Jermy P.Tarcher, Inc.

In a survey of triggers to mystical experiences, Laski notes, "Taken as a whole the people in the groups responded most frequently to *nature*, and next to nature art...by far the most common were water and heights...Mountains...have a substantial tradition as inducing mystical experiences...The greatest religious leaders of the west all had mystical experiences on mountains...Trees and flowers receive comparative frequent mention...Both the flight and the song of birds could be copiously illustrated as triggers to ecstasy..Scent – the odour of flowers, trees, the earth, etc. - is often mentioned..." (pp 187-88).

Muir, John. In *The nature mysticism of John Muir*. Retrieved December 30, 2004 from http://postalproductions.com/spirit-nature/index.html.

"Oh these vast, calm measureless mountain days, inciting at once to work and rest! Days in whose light everything seems equally divine, opening a thousand windows to show us God."

"These blessed mountains are so compactly filled with God's beauty, no petty personal hope or experience has room to be...

"We are now in the mountains and they are in us, kindling enthusiasm, making every nerve quiver, filling every pore and cell of us. Our flesh-and-bone tabernacle seems transparent as glass to the beauty about us, as if truly an inseparable part of it, thrilling with the air and trees, steams and rocks, in the waves of the sun, — a part of all nature, neither old nor young, sick nor well, but immortal...How glorious a conversion, so complete and wholesome it is."

Teasdale, Wayne. (2001). *The mystic heart*. Novato, Ca: The New World Library.

"The term *natural mysticism* expresses the perception and awareness of the numinous reality of the source in, surrounding, and emanating from nature and the cosmos. Everything in this domain is an occasion for the revelation of the divine...When we are caught up in the breathless immensity of a sunrise or sunset, are we not given a glimpse of a hidden revelation?...Natural mysticism is a cosmic revelation of the true face of the natural world" (pp. 174-175).

Thoreau, Henry David. (1906). *The writings of Henry David Thoreau*. Vol 2, p. 313. New York: Houghton Mifflin.

"Standing on the snow-covered plain...I cut my way first through a foot of snow, and then a foot of ice, and open a window under my feet, where, kneeling to drink, I look down into the quiet parlor of the fishes, pervaded by a softened light as through a window of ground glass, and its bright sanded floor the same as in summer; there a perennial waveless serenity reigns as in the amber twilight sky, corresponding to the cool and even temperament of the inhabitants. Heaven is under our feet as well as over our heads."

Etymology

Webster's new world dictionary of the American language. (1956). New York: The World Publishing Company.

"bliss... 1. great joy or happiness. 2. spiritual joy; heavenly rapture..." (p. 157).

"heaven...2. God; Providence. 3. any place of great beauty and pleasure. 4. a state of great happiness. 5. in *theology*, the place where God and his angels are, variously conceived of as the place where the blessed will live after death..." (p. 670).

"paradise... 1. the garden of Eden. 2. heaven. 3. a) any place of great beauty and perfection. b) any place or condition of great happiness" (p. 1060).

Poetry

Barrett-Browning, Elizabeth. (1992) *Aurora Leigh.* Athens: Ohio University Press.

> Earth's crammed with heaven
> And every common bush alive with God.
> Only he who sees takes off his shoes;
> The rest sit around and pluck blackberries (p. 487).

Dickinson, Emily. (1991). *Collected poems.* Philadelphia: Courage Books.

> Eden is that old fashioned House
> We dwell in every day;
> Without suspecting our abode
> Until we drive away.
> How fair, on looking back the Day
> We sauntered from the door,
> Unconscious our returning,
> Discover it no more (p. 370).

> Who has not found the heaven below
> Will fail of it above.
> God's residence is next to mine,
> His furniture is love (p. 224).

Teresa, Sister. Christian Classics Ethereal Library. (n.d.). *My heaven on earth.* In "Poems of St. Teresa, Carmelite of Lisieux, known as the "Little Flower of Jesus". Retrieved August 22, 2006,

from http://www.ccel.org/therese/poems.htm.
All things my love can gain when,
Heart to heart, I pray,
Alone with Jesus Christ in speechless ecstasy.
Beside His alter lest with Him I gladly stay, -
Oh, this is heaven for me!

Wordsworth, William. Intimations of immortality from recollec-
tions of early childhood. In Warren, Robert. (Ed.). (1955). *Six
centuries of great poetry.* New York: Dell Publishing.
There was a time when meadow, grove, and stream,
The earth, and every common sight,
To me did seem
Appareled in celestial light,
The glory and the freshness of a dream.

...trailing clouds of glory do we come
From God, who is our home:
Heaven lies about us in our infancy! (p. 341-2).

Mystical Experiences
Anker-Larsen, Johannes. (1921) With the door open. Erwin and
Pleasaunce von Gaisberg, Trans. In Fremantle, Anne. (1964). *The
Protestant mystics.* London: Weidenfeld and Nicolson).
  "As far back as my memory goes, I can recall a sense of the
Eternal. 'Eternity,' 'heaven,' 'the Kingdom of God,' that was a
reality, which, though I was unable to see it, was nevertheless so
much around me that I could feel sometimes...The 'heaven' or
'Eternity' which surrounded me was so close that it could reach
me with its beneficence...Such, at least, is my recollection of that
time. The earth was the earth, but it lay in the light of Eternity.
Slowly, unperceived, the light grew dimmer, the shadows grew
thick, and became a coarser reality. In the end, Eternity was a day
that had passed away; I had ceased to sense it. But I missed it, and

became religious" (pp 303-4).

"One winter's day I was taking a walk in the Geels forrest...I exalted in *seeing*...My usual sense of ego had gone to sleep like a little child in its crib...I beheld before me a small wood path, so fresh, pure and fairylike that it must have been a path in the Garden of Paradise. There could be no doubt about it, my own joy at the sight of it belonged likewise to Paradise...I was seven years old" (pp. 304-5).

Anonymous. (1921). The prodigal returns. In Fremantle, Anne.(1964). *The Protestant mystics*. London: Weidenfeld and Nicolson).

"The Presence of God was with me day and night, and the world was not the world as I had once known it – a place where men and women fought and sinned and toiled and anguished and wondered horribly the meaning of this mystery of pain and joy, of life an death. The world was become Paradise, and in my heart I cried to all my fellow-souls, 'Why fret and toil, why sweat and anguish for the things of earth when our own God has in His hand such peace and bliss and happiness to give to Every man?" (p. 378).

Bucke, Richard Maurice. (1969). *Cosmic consciousness*. New York: E.P. Dutton and Co.

"It is perhaps impossible for the merely self conscious man to form any conception of what this oncoming of Cosmic Consciousness must be to those who experience it. The man is lifted out of his old self and lives rather in heaven than upon the old earth – more correctly the old earth becomes heaven" (p. 156).

Cohen, Andrew. (2000). *Embracing heaven and earth*. Lenox, MA: Moksha Press.

"Andrew's radical message is, as the title of this book implies, that heaven can be brought to earth – and, in fact, that it is our sacred duty to do so" (p. xvi).

"These five chapters endeavor to bring to light the true meaning and significance of nonduality. They attempt to reveal the deeply mysterious relationship and simultaneous nondifference between heaven and earth, between Enlightenment and the human experience" (p. 75).

"The glory of God is the shattering realization that everything is always perfect..." (p. 95)

Cohen, Andrew. (8/1/04). Quote of the Week. *Heaven on earth*. Retrieved 8/22/06 , from http://www.andrewcohen.org/quote/

It actually is true that the potential for the manifestation of a perfect world, a heavenly realm here on earth, is not dependent upon external circumstances. It is entirely dependent upon us.

Courtois, Flora. (1986). *An experience of enlightenment*. Wheaton, Ill. The Theosophical Publishing House.

In the midst of a profound mystical experience, Flora Courtois recalled, "Passing the campus chapel, I remembered how I had been taught in church to think of myself as here on earth and of God as above and out there, to aspire to heaven as in some future time and place...I knew now that eternity is here always, that there is no higher, no deeper, no separate past or future time or place" (pp. 51-2).

Hoffman, Edward. (1992). *Visions of innocence*. Boston: Shambhala.

"Most fundamentally, it now appears undeniable that some of us (perhaps far more than we suspect) have undergone tremendous peak – even mystical – experiences during our early years. In this respect, conventional psychology and its allied disciplines have painted a badly incomplete portrait of childhood and, by extrapolation, of adulthood" (p. 175).

"Secondly, these reports indicate that a variety of different types of exalted experience are possible during childhood...these can produce a life long interest in mystical teachings and import a sense of abiding security about the human soul and its continuity in a higher world" (p. 176).

Houston, Jean. (1996). *A mythic life.* San Francisco: HarperSanFrancisco.

"I tell my students to close their eyes while I invoke the Dreamtime of paradise. 'As you go deeper in the Dreamtime, tell me what you remember about being in paradise...As the music and my voice carry them deeper, hands begin to go up.'

'I remember when everything was possible and the first smells of autumn would glow inside me.'

'I remember when each moment felt spacious.'

'I remember love, loving, and being loved.'

'I remember being very small and the world being very big and the night being very dark and the stars being very bright and the breeze being very balmy. And someone downstairs that made everything very safe.'

'I remember the moment when I was willing to die because I was part of everything' (pp. 37-38).

Huxley, Aldous. (1963). *The doors of perception.* New York: Harper & Row.

Though controversial, many have discovered the mystical experience of Heaven on Earth while using psychedelic drugs. The distinguished English novelist Aldous Huxley, after ingesting the hallucinogenic peyote derivative mescaline, described,

"I was seeing what Adam had seen on the morning of his creation – the miracle, moment by moment, of naked existence...a bunch of flowers shining with their own inner light and all but quivering under the pressure of the significance with which they were charged;...what rose and iris and carnation so intensely signified was nothing more, and nothing less, than what they were - transience that was yet eternal life...pure Being...the divine source of all existence...Words like 'grace' and 'transfiguration' came to mind...The Beatific Vision, *Sat Chit Ananda*, Being-Awareness-Bliss – for the first time I understood not on the verbal level...but precisely and completely what those prodigious syllables referred to...the sacramental vision of reality...a world where everything shone with the Inner Light, and was infinite in its significance (pp. 17-22).

Johnson, Robert. (1998) *Balancing heaven and earth*. San Francisco: Harper.

"Suddenly I was in a glorious world. It was pure light, gold, radiant, luminous, ecstatically happy, perfectly beautiful, purely tranquil, joy beyond bound...It was all that any mystic ever promised of heaven, and I knew then that I was in possession of the greatest treasure known to humankind. Later in life, I heard the religious scholar Mircea Eliade refer to this magnificent realm as the Golden World, which is exactly right, and I have called it that ever since" (p. 2).

"I drove up to the hills west of Portland...I parked the car and hobbled out onto the promontory just in time for the sunrise. The sun began to inch its way over the horizon with all its glory. The same world I had known at age eleven, the same golden light, the same condensation of pure beauty – it was all there. It was the same world I had lost and mourned several years before...Before, I was a child blundering across a corner of heaven by accident, but now I had the consciousness of a young adult, and my birthright had been restored to me...It lasted for about thirty minutes of clock time, but it was eternity in the heavenly realm...For years my life seemed upended by this glimpse of the divine. Nothing on this earth could fill my hunger for more of the ecstatic experience " (pp. 6-9).

Masefield, John. (1952) So long to learn. In Fremantle, Anne. (1964). *The Protestant mystics*. London: Weidenfeld and Nicolson.

"It is difficult for me to describe the ecstatic bliss of my earliest childhood. All that I looked upon was beautiful, and known by me to be beautiful, but also known by me to be, as it were, only the shadow of something much more beautiful, very, very near, and almost to be reached, where there was nothing but beauty itself in ecstasy, undying, inexhaustible...But from that wonderful hour, I had a life for myself, better than any life of men; and for some years I lived in that life, and could enter it at will, or almost at will, unknown to anybody" (p. 313).

Parsons, Tony. (2000). *As it is*. Carlsbad, CA: InnerDirections Publishing.

"I felt I had been suddenly overtaken and everything took on a new sense. I looked at grass, trees, dogs, and people, moving as before, but now I not only recognized their essence but I was their essence, as they were mine...everything, including me, was enveloped in a deep and all-encompassing love, and in a strange way it seemed that what I saw was also somehow nothing special...it is the norm that is not usually perceived" (p. 32).

"Presence does not bring heaven down to earth or raise earth up to heaven. All is one" (p. 42).

"All is sacred, and we walk and talk and have our time in that which is no less than heaven" (p. 132).

Thoreau, Henry David. (1906). The journal of Henry D.Thoreau. Torrey, Bradford, and Allen, Francis. (Eds.). In Fremantle, Anne.(1964). *The Protestant mystics*. London: Weidenfeld and Nicolson).

"I think that no experience which I have today comes up to, or is comparable with, the experiences of my boyhood...My life was ecstasy. In youth, before I lost any of my senses, I can remember that I was all alive, and inhabited my body with inexpressible satisfaction...This earth was the most glorious musical instrument, and I was audience to its strains...I said to myself, 'There comes into my mind such an indescribable, infinite, all-absorbing, divine, heavenly pleasure...I wondered if a mortal had ever known what I knew" (p. 244).

"If by patience, if by watching, I can secure one new ray of light... the world which was dead prose to me become living and divine, shall I not watch ever?...We are surrounded by a rich and fertile mystery. May we not probe it, pry into it, employ ourselves about it, a little?" (p. 248).

Trevelyan, Katharine. (1963). Through mine own eyes. In Fremantle, Anne. (1964). *The Protestant mystics*. London: Weidenfeld and Nicolson).

"The wonder was beyond anything I have ever read or imagined or heard men speak about. I was Adam walking alone in the first Paradise...Every flower spoke to me, every spider wove a miracle of intricacy for my eyes, every bird understood that here was Heaven come to earth...Every prayer was fulfilled, every possible desire for the whole world consummated; for His Kingdom had come and I had beheld it with my very eyes" (p. 362).

Underhill, Evelyn. (1974). *Mysticism*. New York: Penguin Books.

"Closely connected with the sense of the 'Presence of God,' or power of perceiving the Absolute, is the complementary mark of the illuminated consciousness; the vision of 'a new heaven and a new earth,' or an added significance and reality in the phenomenal world...It takes, as a rule, the form of an enhanced mental lucidity - an abnormal sharpening of the senses - whereby an ineffable radiance, a beauty and a reality never before suspected, are perceived... shining in the meanest things" (p. 254).

"...the visionary sees the whole visible universe transfigured...this illuminated apprehension of things, this cleansing of the doors of perception, is surely what we might expect to occur as man moves towards higher centres of consciousness" (p. 259).

Ordinary Experiences

Robinson, John. (2000). *Ordinary enlightenment.* Unity Village, MO: Unity Books.

"*Ordinary Enlightenment* argues that the Garden is more than a myth, that it actually represents a perception of the ultimate nature of the world. The Garden is found when the world is experienced with senses heightened and wiped clean of mind, time, and self. With naked and intense awareness, we will discover a magical, unspeakably beautiful, luminous and holy place *all around us!*" (p. 45).

Zaleski, Carol & Zaleski, Philip, eds. (2000). *The book of heaven: An anthology of writings from ancient to modern times.* New York: Oxford University Press.

"The most celebrated gates to heaven hinge on death or vision. But what if there were another way to enter? For thousands of years it has been rumored in poetry, song, travel narratives, and social manifestos that heaven may exist right here on earth, accessible to those with the courage or sanctity to seek it out" (p. 313).

Aging

Arrien, Angeles. (2005). *The second half of life.* Boulder: Sounds True, Inc.

"We see the inherent beauty, which is stronger than bodily decline, in older people; we come to understand that we are looking at the radiant largesse of spirit (Heaven) as it comes through the body (Earth)" (p. 76).

Ram Dass. (2000). *Still here: Embracing aging, changing, and dying.*
New York: Riverhead Books.

"...*in the present moment, there is no time.* The gospels of the
world's great religions make reference to this 'eternal present' in
their teaching, instructing seekers after God to look no farther
than where they're standing for the kingdom of heaven. In other
words, eternity is now...The moment is a doorway into eternity"
(p. 135).

Robinson, John. (1997). *Death of a hero, birth of the soul.* Tulsa:
Council Oak Books.

"The Kingdom of Heaven is already here, spread out all over
the earth. It always has been. We are in the garden. We just
misperceive and misunderstand this place...An older man no
longer has the endless future of Spring and Summer. The present
is everything and holds everything. Now is all there is. This
realization can transform his consciousness, for he finds in the
timeless present the eternity he lost years ago" (pp. 310-11).

Robinson, John. (1999). *But where is God? Psychotherapy and the
religious search.* New York: Nova Science Publishers (Troitsa
imprint).

"As the truly mature individual ages and becomes more
permeable to the mystical awareness now leaking through the
soul's membrane, self can open soul and into the divine as the
actual center of consciousness. The divine self increasingly fills
the personality's core and concurrently the world itself is recognized as filled and radiant with Divine Being, for this is the
essential mystical vision. It is this living, wondrous, divine
reality, inside and out, that provides what we need most: joy,
love, purpose, meaning, and courage...Whether we return to
organized religion...or simply learn to live more in everyday
mystical consciousness, our deepening spiritually heals the
artificial split between spirit and matter, psyche and soul, this

world and the 'Kingdom'" (p. 60).

Sinetar, Marsha. (2002). *Don't call me old, I'm just awakening.* New York: Paulist Press.

"Ultimately, spiritual awakening at any age is grace...More and more we simply come awake in God's presence, find that all our doings – our comings and goings – occur in the awareness that we are already engrossed with what will be our occupation in eternity. It's so beautiful it takes my breath away...Many of us ...are no longer aiming for Paradise. To be most precise, after a certain point of awakening, we finally realize: We are Paradise" (p. 161-2).

APPENDIX B

Learning From Heaven's Compass

Introduction

Having learned to experience the Presence, to apply Heaven's Compass to everyday problems and even your self-concept, and to glimpse the divine world of Heaven on Earth, you have acquired some experience with this approach to spiritual growth. As a result, you also may have questions about or be wondering how your experiences compare with that of the hundreds of people who have taken my classes and who previously have used Heaven's Compass. Therefore, this appendix reviews some of the typical questions and experiences that arise in nearly every class I teach on this subject, and then presents some representative examples of successful individual problem-solving using Heaven's Compass. By comparing your experiences with those of others, your understanding of – and confidence with – Heaven's Compass will grow rapidly.

Questions and Answers

Q: I find the first Key, "Stop Thinking," very hard to do. My thoughts just won't stop. What can I do to quiet my mind?

A: People who have tried meditation often describe the frustrating persistence of thought. The mind seems so unruly with its restlessness, distraction and recurring preoccupations. These people, however, don't notice that their mind quiets automatically when they shift into a highly focused sensory task, like threading a needle, the careful painting of trim in a room, climbing a sheer rock wall, examining a diamond for flaws, or practicing a new golf swing. For this reason, I paired the instruction "Stop Thinking," which anyone can do for at least a few seconds, with instructions for sharpening sensory perception

("Intensify Awareness and Perception in the Present" and "Experience the World Exactly As It Is"). Shifting to this focused sensory perception automatically helps quiet the mind because you simply cannot think and sense acutely at the same time. If you are having difficulty with this first Key, practice any intensely sensory activity and keep practicing all four Keys together, because each supports the others and all work synergistically.

Q: I have trouble experiencing the Presence. What's wrong?

A: If you are having trouble with this part, just sit in stillness and silence for a few moments. Remind yourself that stillness and silence not only bring you into the Presence, they *are* the Presence – they represent qualities of Divinity you can experience directly and easily. More than likely, your assumptions and expectations about experiencing God make you discount or overlook such simple forms of sacred experience. If you think silence is just silence, for example, you will look elsewhere for Divinity and miss It.

Next, add other simple elements that make up the experience of Presence, such as focusing on consciousness itself, for that, too, is an aspect of Divinity. Remember, if silence and consciousness are the Presence, and you experience them, you are in fact succeeding.

If you still find this step frustrating, use Heaven's Compass to explore your frustrations. Thus, express the thoughts and feelings involved in the frustration in the World of Man and Darkness quadrants respectively and then dialogue with the Presence about them – even if doubts remain about the authenticity of the dialogue experience. Don't forget to complete the cycle by following the instructions for the Heaven on Earth quadrant. Despite your doubts, if you truly are open and sincere, new insights will arise each time you do this exercise, and they will show you the solution to your dilemma.

Q: I still don't see Heaven on Earth. What's wrong?

A: Whatever you see and experience intensely and without thought *is* the divine world. Expectations and assumptions about what we should see, however, immediately restore the conceptual veil of the World of Man. Worse, they block the experience of wonder, awe and astonishment that transform the everyday world into Heaven on Earth. Practice seeing things without words, ideas or beliefs – really seeing them with intense sensory perception only – and you will discover that the world is far different that what you think. With this kind of seeing, the divine world opens to you naturally.

Q: My glimpses of Heaven on Earth seem to slip away too easily. What's wrong?

A: Glimpses are great! They mean you are beginning to see Heaven on Earth. However, we tend to lose such glimpses for the following reasons:

Thinking: The moment thinking hijacks consciousness again, you're back in the World of Man.

Skepticism: Doubts that whisper, "Heaven on Earth is a ridiculous, stupid or impossible idea," or "This can't really be Heaven; there must be something more," will erase such glimpses and cause you to feel foolish and discouraged instead.

Ambition: The desire to use this new consciousness for personal power, success, fame, or wealth automatically reinstates the World of Man.

Addictions: Compulsive use of drugs, food, sex, and work, as well as the pursuit of perfection and the desire for spiritual highs all restore World of Man illusions, because consciousness becomes clouded by desire, preoccupation and fantasy, or dulled by intoxication.

Buried Emotions: Suppressed emotional pain and depression unconsciously lock you in Darkness. Thus, psychological issues often need to be processed before your consciousness clears enough to see Heaven on Earth. Consider seeing a counselor, therapist or spiritual director to heal any buried emotional distress.

Always work with these barriers using Heaven's Compass to identify the thoughts and emotions involved, and then Stop Thinking, Intensify Awareness and Perception in the Present, Experience the World Exactly As It Is, Come into the Presence Through Your own Presence, and then see the divine world renewed right before your eyes.

Q: What if my behavior begins to seem too weird, eccentric or unacceptable to other people?

A: If you truly live in Heaven on Earth, you will, indeed, change – but for the better. In the World of Man, however, relationships become organized around personal expectations of identity and behavior. As a result, your new behavior might cause some people to become concerned or even angry with you because you no longer seem like who they thought you were, or your new behavior violates their standards of social propriety. Abandoning some of the relationship rules may cause others to fear that you intend to abandon the relationship itself. With these thoughts in mind, here are some ways to respond to other's concerns and criticism:

Stay in the Presence. Trying to explain or argue with others only draws you back into the drama of the false self and false world.

Step back into the experience of no self. Remind yourself, "If I don't exist, then there is no one to defend and no one to be hurt."

If you are hurt or angry, return to Heaven's Compass. Heal yourself first so you can rejoin the other person without sacrificing your mystical consciousness. As you release the problem and return to Heaven on Earth, the conflict may simply disappear (especially if you are no longer reinforcing it with your defensiveness).

Remind yourself that the other person's distress represents their own struggle with the beliefs and illusions of the World of Man. Because this problem stems from the other person's identity, needs and expectations, it can be resolved only through their spiritual growth – not by you. Eventually, the other will realize that your behavior reflects enlightenment not abandonment, representing an opportunity to create a more spiritually advanced relationship. If an insurmountable rigidity underlies the other person's attachment to the World of Man, you may have to choose between staying or growing.

Q: I have trouble connecting with the Presence, but then my dialogue teaches me something new. What's happening?

A: The wonderful part of the dialogue process lies in the fact that it allows another voice to enter consciousness. Your customary voice comes from with the self-concept and can only think in its habitual ways. The "voice" from the Presence, which you hear in the dialogue process, comes from another source and offers new information and perspectives. You can tell your dialogue with the Divine is genuine when it surprises, inspires, teaches, or releases you from old ways of thinking. When this happens, you have, in fact, experienced the Presence. Remember, too, that everyone does this process a little differently. Trust your way and it will continually expand your capacity to experience Divinity.

Q: Sometimes I come out of the process with ideas I already had, and it feels like nothing new has really happened. Why is that?

A: This happens when we cling to our beliefs from the World of Man or remain stuck in Darkness. Reviewing your completed compass, you may find that during the transition into the Presence you never really surrendered your beliefs in the World of Man or your feelings hidden in the Darkness. Perhaps you wanted a preconceived answer or were afraid to risk the discovery or transformation inherent in this journey. Leaving the World of Man and Darkness feels a bit like cutting a kite string. To enter the Presence, you have to let go of the problem and let yourself fly untethered. When you do so, you allow something new to enter your experience and to transform you. If you feel afraid of what you might discover, take that fear into another round of Heaven's Compass, and see what you learn. Take your time doing this. Scary ideas need to be processed slowly, and you need to prepare yourself for real change.

Q: What about the "bad" things that happen? Don't they prove that this cannot be Heaven on Earth?

A: One of the greatest obstacles to finding Heaven on Earth lies with our perception of suffering and evil. People like to claim that disease, disaster, poverty, starvation, abuse, and pain all prove Heaven on Earth is a crazy idea.

Several important issues must be considered when answering this question. First, keep in mind that the moment you make this argument, you exchange the direct perception of Heaven on Earth for the thoughts, stories and fantasies of suffering and evil that make up the World of Man. Rather than argue about suffering and evil, use Heaven's Compass to dissolve your ideas about them. Work on small ideas first to avoid triggering your entire store-house of skepticism, outrage or negativity. Once in the Presence, you will see events previously judged or interpreted in conventional terms in a very different light.

Most importantly, understand that the terrible things we do to each other arise from the beliefs and values of the World of Man and the buried pain and anger they produce in our own Darkness. This cruelty will end when we know where we really are – Heaven on Earth – and, indeed, who we really are – divine beings.

Q: Why do I always have more questions?

A: That is a very important question. The conceptual mind

remains stuck in questions. Every question perpetuates the thinking process and creates more questions. To find and remain in Heaven on Earth, questions must eventually give way to pure perception. Return to the silence of Presence where there exist no questions, no searches for answers, no things to figure out. There you will find Heaven on Earth.

Typical Experiences with Heaven's Compass

Here are examples of the kinds of comments people make as they learn to use Heaven's Compass. See how they match your experience.

"Filling in the quadrants allows me to create space around the problem I started with. Getting it out of my head and onto the paper also gives me much needed distance and perspective so I can move forward and not remain stuck in my head. In the end, the problem no longer seems to own me, because I see it more objectively and less emotionally."

"Putting all my thoughts and feelings in the quadrants helps me to clear out my consciousness so something new can come through. I see, now, that the way I usually work on a problem repeats the same ideas and objectives over and over, actually preventing the discovery of truly new possibilities. I often get very different and valuable information from my dialogues with the Presence."

"I had always separated the psychological and the spiritual. This tool puts them together in a surprisingly effective way. The left side lets me work on thoughts and feelings – the psychological part, and the right side lets me work on the spiritual part where I erase the stories that create my problems. It takes me out of myself, and I see how insignificant my thinking has been. And, after digesting the problem and sorting through it all, Heaven on Earth is the reward."

"Before starting, the exercise seems artificial. And sometimes I feel fearful or apprehensive of what might come out unexpectedly. But, if I do the exercise sincerely, things seem to clear up, and I feel more settled and hopeful, with new ideas about how to live a spiritual life."

"Often when I finish a round with Heaven's Compass, I wonder why the problem was so upsetting to me in the first place, and I see so clearly how my desires, beliefs and expectations are the problem."

"Sometimes I get new ideas in the Presence that I didn't expect, some of which I don't understand at first. If I reflect or meditate on them over time, I gradually discover they hold incredible possibilities for new understanding or change, like seeds of spiritual wisdom that take time to grow in my psyche."

"Once in a while new information comes in from Divinity that seems confusing or scary. Maybe it's too different from my religious beliefs or seems to ask me to change more than I can risk, but when I take that scary thought back through the compass again – and especially when I re-experience the deep peace of Divinity – I realize that it was just another scary idea that disappears like every other idea in the Presence."

"Sometimes I feel like Heaven on Earth is just my imagination, but then I realize that it is, like the experience of Presence, really beyond imagination. When I look at the world as it is and with love and awe, I discover that Heaven on Earth is more real and amazing than anything I could ever think or imagine."

"I've noticed that the revelations that occur in the Presence are totally unique to the individual. As we share our experiences in class, I see how deeply each one reveals the individual's own divine nature and wisdom, that is, their unique expression of God's Being."

"The answers that come from the depths of mystical consciousness are so different from those I generate intellectually. Sometimes they surprise me and sometimes they reveal things I already knew in my soul but had forgotten. It's like I'm recovering wisdom I forgot I had."

"Heaven's Compass doesn't seem to work if I haven't really felt the Presence before I begin my dialogue. Feeling the Presence changes everything. It's as if my old consciousness has been jettisoned and I am once again thrilled with the reality and joy of Divinity. Then whatever happens in the ensuing conversation is startling, refreshing, and helpful."

"The dialogue process itself seems to be really important to the success of Heaven's Compass. It allows another voice to come in, one not associated with my ego, my persona, my goals and views, one that can confront the smallness of my desires and bring me really new information."

"Another insight I've had is this: I don't have to solve all my problems by myself. God will solve them for me if I just get out of the way."

"Doing Heaven's Compass together, the whole class seems to wind up in a peaceful, mellow, contemplative mood, which I sense is a consequence or residue of the experience of Divinity. In this serene consciousness, it's sometimes difficult to speak at all because our individual personalities have not been turned on again."

"Spending time in the Heaven on Earth quadrant at the end of the exercise brings in another form of teaching. The experience of Heaven on Earth shows me more about the real purpose of life, like living in the here and now, and living with love, beauty and peace."

"Sometimes I have to take a problem around Heaven's Compass numerous times or keep coming back to it day after day, like the problem keeps coming back. Really it's my old beliefs, desires and emotions pulling me back in. But even when the problem seems insurmountable, I know it is changing, or I am changing, because little by little I just don't care as much, and I see more clearly what is. Then I know that I am getting ready to make a real change."

"Heaven's Compass is, just like you say, a process of personal revelation. Whatever comes from my dialogue with the Presence feels sacred, feels enlightening and enlivening – literally gifts from God. When I regard what comes from Divinity with this kind of reverence and respect, I am awed at its significance and teaching. I am grateful every time I have this experience."

Examples of Transformation Using Heaven's Compass

Actual experiences with Heaven's Compass provide a rich source of teaching illustrations. Rather than implying that a single correct way exists to do this process, like solving a math problem, they reveal the wonderful diversity of transformational paths and possibilities found in the Presence.

Making Peace with a Messy Bedroom: A Mother's Journey

Terri chose her son's messy bedroom as the problem she wanted to bring through the quadrants of Heaven's Compass. The title of her compass was, "A Messy Bedroom." Here's what she wrote in each quadrant:

World of Man – Brian's room is such a mess. He never picks up his clothes, old food containers are everywhere, the room actually smells. I ask him to at least keep the surfaces clean, and he can't even do that. He's not a bad kid; he's just so lazy about this. I can talk 'till I'm blue in the face and nothing changes. I've tried reasoning, point systems, loss of privileges, nothing works. We just get mad at each other.

Darkness – I feel so angry. I feel so disrespected. I feel like a failure. I feel like a maid. I hate this situation. And I hate having to clean up his messes. I feel like screaming, then I feel like crying. I feel like a crappy mother.

Divinity – Terri: "God, thank you for being here. In your presence, none of this really matters. In your presence, I'm just so happy to be alive. Only peace remains and joy and relief, but still I have to ask, 'What do I do about Brian's room and his behavior? What am I supposed to do?'"

Presence: "Let go of your harping and worry. It is only a stage on his journey. What matters is what a beautiful boy he is. Can you see his sweetness, his beauty, his budding manhood. You are watching a miracle. You are part of a miracle happening. Be happy that he is such a wonderful child."

Terri: "God that feels so liberating, but aren't I supposed to be teaching him responsibility or cleanliness or something like that?"

Presence: "Those are concepts only – artificial ones, ones the culture imposes. They are ideas forced on the becoming of a soul. He'll work it out when his unfolding reaches the next level. It will just happen. Love what he is becoming. Love this stage of his becoming. Everything has a developmental purpose."

Terri: "So I just leave him alone?"

Presence: "No, love him unconditionally. Love everything about him. Be happy with all that he is. His room is just a passing phenomenon, but every part of the mess is part of his beauty.

Experience the love that I am, and celebrate this time of his life – it will not last forever. It is to be cherished."

Terri: "Oh, thank you, God. I feel so unburdened, and this feels so much better than fighting a losing, stupid fight with him that only makes us all unhappy. I feel so much freedom now."

Heaven on Earth – "If this were Heaven on Earth, then…" each and every thing on his floor and on his desk and in his dirty clothes pile is imminent with God, is filled with You, God, is made of you. And everything is so wonderful, like a work of art – colors and shapes and arrangements and smells. Yes, some of it needs to be cleaned for health reasons, but I don't mind. Let him find his own way of solving this problem. This world, just as it is, is so full and wonderful and rich and pregnant with you, Lord. How can I be unhappy?

Review — Looking at the four quadrants, I realize that the problem was one I was making, and I was making myself crazy. A lot of it was being worried about what other people would think of me as a mother. Now I really don't care what anyone thinks. I feel so free. I am free to do what I love most, which is to love him and laugh at what's funny about this stage and let the whole thing go.

A Teacher Learns About Controlling His Temper in Class

Tom teaches fourth grade. He chose "Controlling my temper" as the title of the problem he wanted to resolve in Heaven's Compass. Here is his written exercise:

World of Man – I need to contain my temper in class. It's not that I act out, it's just that the kids can really drive me up the wall. Sometimes they come at me so intensely and so suddenly that I recoil, feel invaded and then struggle to keep from getting really angry. After I'm upset, I don't function well for a while. I've tried everything, like meditating and counting to 10, but I'm not there yet.

Darkness – This problem makes me feel really bad about

myself and my teaching, like I'm letting the kids down and not doing my best, but I get so mad. I especially hate it when hyper little boys start racing around and don't heed my instructions to stop or follow directions. I just feel like screaming at them to stop.

Divinity – Tom: "God, I don't know what to do. Show me the way."

God: "Try deflecting their energy like a football player or martial arts expert."

Tom: "I don't know what you mean. How do I do that?"

Presence: "Use their energy instead of reacting to it. Let it go by you, not through you."

Tom: "That's really interesting, but I still don't understand. I'm intrigued and puzzled."

Presence: "Take this idea to class with you, and see what you learn."

Heaven on Earth – "If this were Heaven on Earth, then..." this is a fascinating problem. Now it's not so upsetting, rather it's some kind of beautiful dance that I can learn to flow with. I can be part of the dance, moving with, instead of against, its energies, like a ballet. I can't wait to see what happens if I bring Heaven into my classroom, especially if I bring the love and patience I feel now to my experience of the kids. If this were Heaven on Earth, then it's a wonderful challenge, and I love these kids in a way I couldn't before. I'm ready to see how the principle of deflection might work.

Review – My problem has changed from a never-ending stressful situation that made me feel bad to a really interesting dance that I think I can learn from. And it's not about me, it's about God and how God might show me what he means by deflection and how I can use it. I'm already trying to imagine how it might work.

Reconciling with a Brother

Mary had been very close to her brother as a young child. During school years, however, they had drifted apart and had been estranged for years. She called her compass, "Looking for my brother."

World of Man – All through our early years, we played endlessly together and were each other's best friend. Then, in school, we seemed to go different ways. Now we're like two insulated wires – we don't connect. We're polite, but it seems so dead between us.

Darkness – All sorts of feelings come up as I think about him – sadness, regret, anger, bitterness, helplessness, and guilt. I'm afraid to see him now because it seems so hopeless.

Divinity – When I came into the Presence, I felt so much love, and I realized that this love has no boundaries or limits in time or space. I began to feel this love include me and then move all the way to Southern California where he lives. I felt it surround him, and then I relaxed. I knew I still loved him and it would be okay. (*Author's Note:* Notice that Mary's transformation comes simply from the experience of Presence; she doesn't even write a dialogue.)

Heaven on Earth – "If this were Heaven on Earth, then…" we would be close again. I suddenly pictured us walking together again down a country road holding hands. It was so wonderful. I now know that whatever happens, my feelings have changed and that I can hold him in my heart with love now. I think that love will gradually change us, melt our differences. I think he will feel this love somehow, and that we will begin to come back together. I am no longer afraid.

Review – My biggest problem, I realize, was the belief that the problem was hopeless. When that dissolved in the Presence and love flowed through again, I felt so much better. I know that this love will heal me and in time melt that strain between us. And even if my brother can't let go psychologically, my love will heal our relationship on a spiritual level.

Healing a Mother Wound

Planning a vacation with her mother, June discovered an old wound that threatened the whole trip. Through the stages of Heaven's Compass, she found a deeply spiritual solution to this problem. She called her compass, "My Mother." Here is what she wrote on the Compass:

World of Man – Three years ago I learned that Mom thought I was trying to come between her and Bill, my brother. She told me she didn't want me to drive her to see him, because she wanted her own time with him and didn't want me there. It was the first time I realized that she was jealous and resented me, the first time I doubted her love for me.

Darkness – I felt shocked, hurt, heartbroken, empty, betrayed, deluded, gullible, righteous, outraged. I felt my mother had never loved me in the way I thought she had and that our relationship had never been what I thought it was – that, in fact, she didn't like me at all.

Divinity – June. "I feel devastated, afraid to re-encounter my mother and especially afraid to be with her in Bill's presence."

Presence: "Let what will happen, happen. You cannot be harmed by this. Love is not, cannot be, diminished by human belief or human mistakes. The love of your mother for you, and you for her, is maximal, everlasting regardless of human happenings. Live in this knowledge. Allow her humanness/your humanness, in a spirit of compassion, secure in the knowledge that Love is inviolate, unaffected, eternal. It cannot be lost or gained, but is ever and always yours and hers."

Heaven on Earth – "If this were Heaven on Earth, then..." Love would be my only awareness, my state of Being, my gracious acceptance of all possible events and outcomes, encompassed by my awareness that this has not changed my Reality at all, regardless of who or what is involved."

Review – Events come and go. How I am in them is a choice. I can invent them as problems or move through them. In the end, I can't really make anything happen, but if I am in the Presence, God will unfold the perfect solution, if I let Him.

Making This Book A Success

I end with a personal example. Near the beginning of a long editing process, I began to wonder if this book would ever be successful. Feeling tired and discouraged, I turned again to Heaven's Compass and titled this round, "What's the point?" Here's what I wrote:

World of Man – I have worked so hard on this book for so many years, revising it so many times and receiving so many rejections. I think Heaven's Compass is an amazing process, my classes and clients like it, but I can't convince anyone of its value at the publishing level. Am I crazy to continue? Is this just an exercise in narcissism, a defense against the reality of aging, a way to fill my time in retirement? Why am I doing this? Is this just an old man clinging to dreams of life's purpose and relevance?

Darkness – I feel tired and discouraged. I fear this whole thing will end up being a waste of time and money, time I should be spending giving back to the world in more direct and practical ways, in volunteer service, time with my children and grand-children, political activities. I feel so beaten down. Why do I keep going? Why am I here?

Divinity – John: "Hello God, are you here?"

Presence: "Always."

John: "Oh God, thank you for being here. It feels so good to be close to you again. You are all I need. I love how it feels to be with you. So, I have come to ask you why I am still working on this book. Am I wasting my time? Is this just some old vanity or fear of getting old? Does this make any sense? Please help me see what I am doing."

Presence: "Be happy, John. None of that matters. You are doing this because it makes you happy, because it is your unfolding. It's the way your vine grows, fed and fueled by me. It is your way."

John: "But will it ever see the light of day? Will it ever make a difference in the world?"

Presence: "It already has. Your seed has been planted. It's growing everywhere. The world changes not just by outer events but by vision, intention and love. Yours are spreading all through the world. Measure success by the love you feel not by the standards in the World of Man. It is like putting a drop of ink in a tank of clear water: It spreads everywhere, touching every corner and atom."

John: "But I don't see it changing the world. Everything keeps getting more violent, more painful, more foolish, more destructive. Where is the impact?"

Presence: "There is an invisible world that, like the water in the tank, is everywhere. What you have created touches that world, and one day will change it. In the meantime, this work will find a publisher and disseminate into the World of Man. You will see. The seed was good. It is enough. This is a wonderful force of spirit and life. Trust what I have created through you."

John: What should I do?"

Presence: "Let me do this for you. It is why I am here. Just trust this life I have given you. I am the farmer. I am the Earth. It will grow. Be the vine."

Heaven on Earth – "If this were Heaven on Earth, then…" I am so happy. Then everything is as it should be. All is perfect. And the joy of this process is the seed that spreads its goodness. Heaven works differently than the World of Man. This is enough. I can feel it flowing everywhere. It is already successful. It is my contribution to the whole. I am so grateful for this opportunity to love in the way I was meant to love. Thank you, God. Thank you.

Review – The lesson in this dialogue seems so hard to get sometimes. The barriers and doubts come from me, not from God. The joy and love and creativity I experience in this process flow from God and contribute to the expansion and awakening of Creation. The "problem" arises from thoughts that constrict, devalue or shatter this flow. The "problem" is always me.

Conclusions

Working with Heaven's Compass represents a spiritual practice that takes time and experience to master. Be assured that your competency will grow as you practice and that the One guiding you will continue to teach you and to expand your skills.

www.johnrobinson.org

BOOKS

O is a symbol of the world, of oneness and unity. In different cultures it also means the "eye", symbolizing knowledge and insight. We aim to publish books that are accessible, constructive and that challenge accepted opinion, both that of academia and the "moral majority".

Our books are available in all good English language bookstores worldwide. If you don't see the book on the shelves ask the bookstore to order it for you, quoting the ISBN number and title. Alternatively you can order online (all major online retail sites carry our titles) or contact the distributor in the relevant country, listed on the copyright page.

See our website **www.o-books.net** for a full list of over 400 titles, growing by 100 a year.

And tune in to myspiritradio.com for our book review radio show, hosted by June-Elleni Laine, where you can listen to the authors discussing their books.

MySpiritRadio